MW00446243

BOLTON

BOLTON

HISTORIC TALES

HANS DePOLD

FOREWORD *by* PAMELA SAWYER

Charleston · London

THE
History
PRESS

Published by The History Press
Charleston, SC 29403
www.historypress.net

Copyright © 2008 by Hans DePold
All rights reserved

First published 2008

Manufactured in the United States

ISBN 978.1.59629.563.6

Library of Congress Cataloging-in-Publication Data

De Pold, Hans.
Bolton : historic tales / Hans DePold.
p. cm.
ISBN 978-1-59629-563-6
1. Bolton (Conn.)--History. I. Title.
CT104.B55D4 2008
974.6'43--dc22

2008037203

Notice: The information in this book is true and complete to the best of our knowledge. It is offered without guarantee on the part of the author or The History Press. The author and The History Press disclaim all liability in connection with the use of this book.

All rights reserved. No part of this book may be reproduced or transmitted in any form whatsoever without prior written permission from the publisher except in the case of brief quotations embodied in critical articles and reviews.

*To the many people and organizations struggling to have
Washington and Rochambeau recognized with a National Historic Trail
on their Revolutionary Route from Newport, Rhode Island,
to Yorktown, Virginia.*

Contents

Contents

Foreword

I grew up in Providence, not far from Rochambeau Avenue. Wonderful childhood memories include getting my first library card at Rochambeau Library and then reading a Benjamin Franklin biography repeatedly. But growing up in a city made me long for country life, and at a young age I decided I would raise my own family in a quiet town.

For me, Bolton is that place. This small town has undergone a transformation since the days of Franklin. At that time, it was a farming community with bare hills and stone walls that crisscrossed the countryside. Today it's a lushly treed suburban area where residents find pride in their schools and the town's community spirit.

With good fortune, I was elected to state public office, and I relished this opportunity to help my community. But right away I was in the middle of a thirty-year-old problem that nagged five governors and countless other state employees and officials.

I didn't know it at the time, but considering this troublesome transportation issue would further my love affair for this town in which I raised my children.

Should the state complete a section of expressway between Hartford and Providence? The gap stood at eleven miles, and there was talk about building a meatier highway that would cross through Bolton. Route 6 bridged the gap for years, but had become infamously hazardous. Reader's Digest had dubbed it the second-most "dangerous road in America," and it ran through two towns in my legislative district.

That prompted my personal Route 6 study. I found its history enthralling. It started out as a cart path that connected farms in the Hop River area, and it was a documented "Revolutionary Road," used by heroes such as comte de Rochambeau. My childhood idol, Franklin, also used it, as did our war general, George Washington. He met with the French to plan the decisive Battle of Yorktown.

I discovered these facts through research done by a passionate advocate who wanted to preserve the road's historical record as well as the town's. Hans DePold has a home on the old state road, and he delved into a rich set of facts that led him deep into Bolton's history—well before and well after the Revolution made its imprint here.

Hans had an advantage: he understood French. He studied original maps and records that described this country's relationship with France. Revolutionaries here depended on the support of French troops to push the dream of American independence toward reality.

In the early 1990s, Hans persuaded me to secure state funding for archaeological work along the Washington-Rochambeau Revolutionary Route (W3R) in Connecticut to mark its place in history. The success earned me a moniker: "Godmother of the W3R."

Hans DePold's in-depth study of the Revolutionary War era led to research of many other local historical events, which he brought to life for our townspeople through articles in the *Bolton Community News*. This book shows his passion for our history.

We are all richer for his research.

State Representative Pamela Sawyer

Preface

I would never have had the opportunity to write this book were it not for the Army Corps of Engineers' proposal to put a highway through the centers of Bolton and Andover, Connecticut. Almost as an afterthought of a $20 million highway study, they decided to include input from the communities that were affected. I was selected to be the Bolton Economic Development Commission representative on the ad hoc committee that the Department of Transportation (DOT) created.

The concept of heritage preservation–based tourism was new, but we could see that the concept was successfully applied in Massachusetts in the 1970s. At the time, Bolton had only one house on the National Register of Historic Places, with no historical society or other group representing heritage. Our town municipal historian had been the DOT's top Connecticut road and highway historian, and he taught me what he knew about the roads and highways in and around Bolton. However, he was planning to move, so he asked me to represent him at the meetings.

We created an Intercommunity Historic Resources Committee, and at the very first meeting in Andover, Lorraine Busque loaned me her book on the French campaigns during the America Revolution. Everyone had believed the important Revolutionary War encampments in Bolton were not going to be affected. As soon as I saw the French map of Camp Five, I knew the real campsite was half a mile north of where the local maps showed it to be, and it was near the center of town on the farm that the proposed highway would split in two.

To establish the correct location, I placed the French map of Camp Five next to a topographical map of the site and presented it to the DOT ad hoc committee. While those representing state heritage agreed that it was probably true, they said it would take a long and expensive study to prove it. I had lived in East Hartford and remembered that while I was on the East Hartford Town Council, the French Revolutionary War Camp Six was being paved over, and no one came forward to defend it. So we took a more active approach to defend this central part of Bolton's heritage. My wife (the Bolton town clerk) and I wrote and presented the evidence directly to the French ambassador in Washington, D.C., and to the French consul in New York City, and asked them (if they agreed) to bring this fact to the attention of Connecticut Governor Rowland, to whom the DOT and the Historic Preservation Commission reported. To our surprise, they both wrote back within a few weeks and said they had done it. The oldest running U.S. newspaper, the *Hartford Courant*, carried headlines saying that the French government asked for the preservation of the Franco-American Revolutionary War site. I gave a copy of the map to Richard Rose, the farmer who owned Camp Five. A few weeks later, he asked me to tell the Bolton Economic Development Commission that he would like to preserve the farm heritage and would be willing to sell the farm to the town. I was appointed Bolton municipal historian right about then.

From that point on, interest and knowledge about our heritage began to snowball. I had the opportunity to submit the first draft description for a Washington-Rochambeau Revolutionary Route (W3R) study for a state bill. Representative Pamela Sawyer's legislation for the study of W3R passed. The Connecticut study and archaeological digs verified the location of Camp Five and all the other Connecticut Revolutionary War campsites along the W3R. We held a well-attended meeting in September 1998, where the report on the archaeological discoveries was discussed and we circulated two volunteer lists. After the meeting, we immediately held short meetings to create the Bolton Historical Society and the Friends of the Rose Farm to advocate the purchase of the Rose Farm.

The Connecticut Society of the Sons of the American Revolution provided a website to keep all the Revolutionary Road newsletters I was writing. I was also writing articles for newspapers and for the *Bolton Community News*, and many of the articles were going on the *Bolton Community News* website.

State Representative Pamela Sawyer came back from a vacation trip to England and was excited because the actor who portrayed George Washington's father at their original English estate knew that she was the Connecticut legislator who introduced the Connecticut W3R study bill. He was one of our worldwide newsletter readers.

The Governor's Francophone Commission and the French veterans group, Le Souvenir Francaise, were soon involved, and I provided a list of active and higher-placed W3R newsletter subscribers in the nine states along the Revolutionary Route. The first national W3R organization was born in December 1999.

In early 2000, at a packed Bolton town meeting, 97 percent voted to purchase the historic farm with the Revolutionary War military encampments.

A little later in 2000, Democratic State Central Committee member Patricia Morianos arranged a meeting in Bolton to discuss possible W3R federal legislation with our freshman congressman, John B Larson. He agreed, and introduced and championed the national study bill to define the interstate route and make a recommendation on the viability of creating a Washington-Rochambeau Revolutionary Route National Historic Trail (W3R NHT). The bill passed both houses of Congress unanimously, and the National Park Service (NPS) completed their study in 2007. The study recommended that the W3R NHT be designated by Congress. The bill is up for a vote this year.

This book explores Bolton's history that revolved around the unique Native American mountain pass called Bolton Notch. Bolton Notch made Bolton the eastern gateway into the Connecticut valley in colonial times. This book covers exciting events and stages of change that are leading Bolton to be reborn as the western gateway from the Connecticut valley into the scenic "Quiet Corner of Connecticut."

Acknowledgements

Thank you to Eleanor Preuss, Diane Danna, Ruth Treat, Marilyn Fiano, Paula Morra, Marjorie Martin and Beverly Logan for taking the time to look for and bring in photos of Bolton. Other historical societies, notably Manchester and Tolland, also contributed photos, postcards and illustrations.

I also wish to thank Ann Maulucci, Bonnie Massey, Dorothy Krause, Eileen Stanley, John Toomey and Steven Arnold from the Bolton Historical Society for all their efforts in this endeavor, and especially for their help organizing photographs.

I am grateful to Genevieve Robb and Judith Lodi for their interest and enthusiasm for this book, and for the many photos each provided to bring this project to a successful conclusion. Elna Dimock was a much-valued source of information about Bolton's past—thank you.

This book would not have been possible without the many contributions of my wife and history partner, Susan, town clerk of Bolton, for which I am most appreciative.

Thank you to Saunders Robinson of The History Press for the advice, guidance and patient management of this project.

Artists Susan Bosworth and Hans Weiss and photographer Kyle Dooman contributed some of their work to this book, for which I thank them.

Soon after I began studying the heritage of Bolton, State Representative Pamela Sawyer sponsored legislation that funded research and documentation of the Washington-Rochambeau Revolutionary Route in Connecticut and in particular in the Town of Bolton. Congressman John Larson and Senators

ACKNOWLEDGEMENTS

Joseph Lieberman and Thomas Dodd sponsored the federal legislation that funded research and documentation of W3R heritage in all the original American colonies. I thank each of them for their continued interest and support of legislation that should soon make the Washington-Rochambeau Revolutionary Route National Historic Trail a reality managed by the National Park Service.

I am deeply indebted to the *Bolton Community News* and its editor, Eileen Stanley, for giving local history an important place in her excellent newspaper and website. I am also indebted to the Connecticut Society of the Sons of the American Revolution and their webmaster, Steven Shaw, for the cogent, dependable, worldwide publicity that they have given to the Revolutionary Road.

Thanks also go to Arnold Carlson of the Coventry Historical Society, Russ Wirtalla of the Connecticut Sons of the American Revolution, Colonel Serge Gabriel of Le Souvenir Francais and Jay Jackson of the Society of the Cincinnati, which has provided numerous grants for the W3R and Bolton historical research.

The late Marian "Rusty" Kelsey was chairman of the Economic Development Commission in the 1990s, when it was the first town commission to recommend the purchase of the Rose Farm. She had the wonderful ability to look simultaneously to the past and to the future, all for the good of Bolton.

Extra special thanks also go to the following for their continuing efforts to preserve the natural and historic heritage of Bolton: State Senator Mary Ann Handley, Pat Morianos, David Loda, Rod Parlee, Robert Morra, Nancy Soma, Joshua Hawks-Ladds, Joyce Stille, Marge and Bert Flynn, Ruth Mensing, Gwen Marrion, Richard Treat, Beth Harney, Sandra Pierog, Larry Pesce, Arlene Fiano and the members of the Bolton Women's Club. Pat Morianos has had a greater role in preserving the natural and historic heritage of Bolton than most people can imagine.

Part I

The Dawn of Bolton

Mundo Wigo, the Creator Is Good

Bolton Notch Mountain forms the watershed divide for the Connecticut and Thames Rivers, and at its summit, suspended some one hundred feet above the Rails to Trails greenway, there is a pond. A well-worn path wends its way around the pond lined with thin bands of high-bush blueberry, mountain laurel, winterberry and sweet pepper bush. The pond is fed by rainwater and has no outlet.

Many of our residents climb the notch, especially in October, when after a light rain the fall colors are spectacular. They climb the mountain to be dazzled by the lemon, orange and raspberry colors. Here on the craggy outcrop of rock is the divide between the ancient Podunk tribal hunting lands to the west, and the Mohegan hunting lands to the east. Using mountains as landmarks, Native Americans crisscrossed Connecticut on well-worn paths. These footpaths became the first roads connecting settlements. Down below is the notch, through which major Mohegan trails converged and later became Ye Olde Connecticut Path, running from the Massachusetts Bay Colony to the Hartford Colony. It was the eastern gateway to the Connecticut valley.

The Mohegan used Bolton Notch as their lookout for unexpected visitors from the east or west. From there, fleet-footed runners were sent to inform the wise and mighty Uncas, the Mohegan sachem (chief). The mountain itself has several caves created by the effect of gradual seepage from the pond at the top of the notch.

The spirits of Native Americans were believed to inhabit important places, and if we close our eyes while standing on top of the notch, we can hear the rustling of the leaves where Mohegan walked like the wind in what has been described as continuous forest, with trees up to two hundred feet tall and six feet in diameter. Their moccasins left no sounds on the forest floor. Wildlife abounded, with wolves, otters, deer, bears, rattlesnakes and turkeys that could be caught easily. They respected all life forms and hunted only out of necessity.

They were storytellers. At the campfire, they reflected on their expanding awareness of the beautiful garden in which they lived. It was a place of life and sustenance, where they stood as the guardians and stewards of the land and of all life. These Native Americans farmed, traded, hunted and gathered foods, primarily near the many sources of water. They lived in small groups of several hundred or fewer, and had several languages and dialects.

They chose to live in harmony with all of God's creations. The Native American painted his face to appear savage and frightening. War was often won with frightening gestures, savage threats, bluster and noise. Peace was

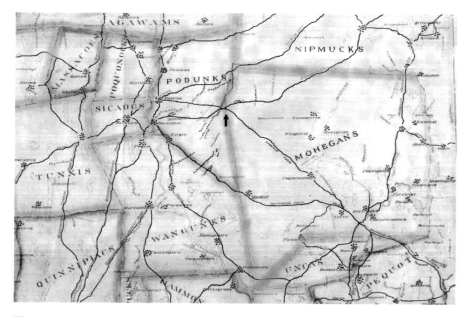

The map of early Connecticut tribes and trails shows the region that became Bolton was the home of Mohegan and Podunk tribes. The importance and growth of Bolton was predestined by the important nexus of trails through Bolton Notch (shown by the arrow) from the south and east into the center of Connecticut. These paths became the paths of later colonization and colonial trade.

often achieved by convincing the other group to leave the confrontation and perhaps settle some place else.

Originally an Algonquin tribe, the Pequot/Mohegan came from the upper Hudson River valley in New York. During a mini ice age sometime around 1500 BC, they left that area and fought their way to the Thames River valley in southeastern Connecticut.

They called Bolton Notch "Saqumsketuck" (songk-ompsk-it-auke), meaning a "place of hard rock," referring to the fact that the stone there was excellent for making sharp axes, lance heads and grinding tools. The Bolton lakes did not exist at that time. Looking more like the Florida Everglades, the area was a cedar swamp. At the west side of the swamp was a large work area with great masses of stone flakes from toolmaking.

The early 1600s was a critical time of change for Connecticut tribes. The pressure from rapidly expanding European settlements created competition for land and resources, while the diseases from Asia and Africa that once decimated Europe were now decimating Native American populations. The Native American tribes still lived closely in cold communal lodges and wore

Cedar Swamp was a summer camp for the Mohegan, where they would fashion stone tools and weapons from nearby Bolton Notch stone.

little more than blankets in winter. Once sick, their living conditions offered them little hope of surviving. From 1616 to 1619, an epidemic spread through the Native American tribes called "the Great Dying." An estimated 70 percent to 90 percent of the native population died from European diseases ranging from diphtheria to influenza, smallpox (the fever), the plague (putrid fever) and tuberculosis (coughing blood). There was no understanding of diseases then, but Jesuit Father Pierre Biard reported in 1614 of the Native Americans: "They are astonished and often complain that, since the French mingle with them and carry on trade with them, they are dying fast, and the population is thinning out."

In addition to refugee European colonists, the English, Dutch and French aristocracies were present in America for business purposes. All of the Native Americans sought trade alliances with the European tribes. The Mahican (New York) and the Pequot (Connecticut) allied themselves to the Dutch. The Mohegan (Connecticut) and the Mohawk (New York) allied with the English. These were economic alliances of nations that transcended color.

WUNNEE AND SQUAW CAVE

The first European access to the interior of America was via the coastal rivers using ocean sailing ships. The name "Connecticut" is Native American for the "Land of the Long River." The first Native American encounter with Europeans in Connecticut was with the Dutch navigator Adrian Block in 1614. Between 1614 and 1624, the Dutch fur trade along the banks of the Connecticut reached ten thousand pelts annually. In 1634, a Dutch trading ship, the *Fortune*, docked at Adrian's Landing on the Connecticut River to trade with the Native Americans for furs. One of the crew, Peter Hager, happened to be taken by the beauty of the Podunk Indian princess, Wunneetunah. Her father, the sachem, approved and welcomed Peter into the Podunk community. Peter decided to stay with the Podunk tribe and marry the princess according to the Podunk custom.

Later that year, Peter and "Wunnee" decided to also seek a Christian marriage, so they walked to the Bay Colony (Boston) to be married. In the Bay Colony, Peter was arrested because intermarriage with Native Americans was then illegal. He was sentenced to the pillory stocks, which locked the feet and hands in a fixed position to display and shame the guilty person. That night, Wunneetunah and her mother freed Peter and they fled the Bay Colony. Two Puritans caught up with them. While Peter defended his wife and mother-in-law, one of the Puritans fell and hit his head on a rock and died. Peter and Wunnee now had to go into hiding.

They lived for a while at what became know as Wickham Park (East Hartford), and were often seen in the area now called Love Lane. In those earlier days, it went through a pine grove. Peter and Wunnee next fled to a deep ravine that is now Center Spring Park (Manchester). The couple, though, would not be safe there for long either. They fled to what is now called Squaw's Cave at Bolton Notch, in Mohegan territory. They would hunt and fish in the cedar swamp area and forage nuts and berries. One day a bounty hunter shot Peter, but Peter managed to hide in the cave, where he died. Several Englishmen came but they never found Peter's body. The cave is blocked now, but was said to lead deep into the mountain and to a secret exit on the other side.

The widow Wunneetunah returned to her family by the Podunk River and never married again. She eventually became a maid to an English family in Windsor, where she is buried in an old Windsor cemetery. Her tombstone reads, "Here lies One Hage [Wunee Hager], Indian Princess."

THE PEQUOT WAR

The Pequot tribe was once ruled by the sachem Tatobem (Wopigwooit). The Pequot had sought to be the middlemen in the trade with the Dutch, and they were caught killing other Native Americans who tried to contact the Dutch directly. In an incident in 1631, at the Dutch trading post at Adrian's Landing (present-day Hartford), the Dutch killed Tatobem. Tatobem's son, Sassacus, still remained loyal to the Dutch, but Sassacus's brother-in-law, Uncas, no longer believed the Dutch to be as trustworthy as the English.

The name Uncas is derived from Wonkus (Fox). He was the son of Owenoco, a Mohegan chief. In 1626, Uncas married Tatobem's daughter and became one of the Pequot leaders. Uncas knew that survival was not easy, and believed that the great creator Mundo would decide if the European tribes would survive. When he realized that the English were there to stay, Uncas took action to make sure that the Mohegan tribe would survive with them.

When the Pequot tribe chose Sassacus to be their new leader in 1633, Uncas and his followers separated from the main body to become the Mohegan. Uncas lived for a while with the Narragansett, who were another former Algonquin tribe that settled adjacent to the Pequot in the bay area of Rhode Island. The Mohegan traded with the English from the Bay Colony area. They, along with the Podunk and other small river tribes, encouraged

Trading, hunting, gathering and limited farming was a way of life for many tribes. Noted Connecticut artist Hans Weiss sketched an individual and two trading Native Americans on location at a Connecticut powwow and painted them at his studio.

the English to settle near the Dutch trading post. Uncas established his new Indian nation to the north of the main Pequot settlements, and they called their homeland Moheganeak. Many Mattabesic, Nipmuc and members of other tribes joined the Mohegan when they saw that Uncas was true to Native American traditions.

The incursion of Europeans dramatically altered things. Connecticut's first English settlement was Windsor, established in 1633. In 1634, trader John Oldham and three companions were the first Englishmen to set foot in what is now Bolton as they made their way on what would become known as the Olde Connecticut Path, a series of prehistoric Native American trading and hunting paths that connected the Massachusetts Bay area and central Connecticut. John Oldham directly helped the English settle in Wethersfield and opened the English route through Bolton for colonization of Connecticut. The English set up a trading post at Windsor to divert trade from the Dutch and put them out of business.

In 1634, the Western Niantic, in self-defense, killed John Stone and seven of his crewmen when Stone tried to capture and enslave some of their tribe. The English considered the deaths a dangerous precedent.

In 1636, Reverend Thomas Hooker led Puritan followers from Massachusetts on the Olde Connecticut path through Bolton to settle in

Hartford, becoming the first major English settlement in Connecticut and establishing a military presence and a seat of government with the Hartford Court. The Pequot resented the English because they drove out the Dutch, so the Pequot began harassing and intimidating the new English settlers and the river tribes that had invited the English. The powerful Mohawk nation from the Hudson and Mohawk River valleys were the traditional peacekeepers for the tribes of the Connecticut valley that the Pequot were terrorizing.

By May 1636, the colonists had had enough of Pequot killings. A General Court was convened in Hartford. The unanimous result: "It is ordered that there shall be an offensive war against the Pequots." The Pequot immediately called upon all tribes to unite with them, but not a single Native American tribe supported them. The Narragansett were already skirmishing with the Pequot.

The breaking point came on July 20, 1636, when it was reported that the Pequot killed John Oldham. Many English then demanded that the Pequot involved be punished. Then the Pequot killed eight English farmers, three women and kidnapped two teenage girls in one more raid.

Finally, in 1637, Captain John Mason convinced Uncas to join forces with the English in a plan to attack the Pequot. When Uncas brought his one hundred best warriors through Bolton Notch to join the English, the English soldiers numbered ninety. The English, however, expected many more warriors and were not satisfied with what they perceived as a lack of enthusiastic Mohegan support for punishing the Pequot. Mason was concerned that they might not have sufficient strength to win, so he sailed to pick up the Narragansett Sachem, Miantonomo, and a few hundred of his warriors, who were mortal enemies of the Pequot. The combined force surrounded the Pequot village at Missituk (now Mystic) while Sassacus and most of his warriors were out attacking English settlers and neighboring tribes.

It is estimated that Sassacus had murdered about thirty settlers before the English set fire to the largest Pequot camp and killed all that tried to escape. Over five hundred Pequot men, women and children perished at Missituk. The Mohegan and the Narragansett had never experienced European total warfare before, so they had not previously seen such disregard for innocent human life. Uncas was visibly disturbed by the destruction, and John Mason recorded that he believed Uncas said that it was evil. But the killing only whetted Miantonomo's thirst for killing the Pequot.

Sassacus arrived too late to save his village, and fled to New York with his warriors, where the Mohawk captured and killed most of them. The

Mohawk cut off Sassacus's head and sent it to Hartford as a gesture of friendship.

The English first wanted to sell the defeated Pequot as slaves for the sugar cane plantations, where the average slave would be worked to death within seven years. Uncas interceded and asked that the Pequot tribe be merged with the Mohegan to create a large, stable and dependable ally of the English. The English initially accepted Uncas's proposal and Uncas brought peace and stability to Connecticut in 1637. Pequot and Western Niantic tribes were placed under the guardianship of Uncas, creating a combined population of about three thousand. Within a few years, the Pequot were once again free people in Moheganeak.

But Uncas was reprimanded and threatened with arrest while visiting the Massachusetts Bay Colony because he treated the Pequot as equals, not as slaves. The English then sought to weaken the Mohegan by dividing the Pequot from the Mohegan. To do that, they first required the Pequot to engage in slave labor, making wampum as tribute for the English. The hardship caused the Pequot to resent their Mohegan guardians. That gave the English the opportunity several years later to reprimand the Mohegan for being too harsh on the Pequot, and provided a justification to divide the Pequot off as two small tribes, thereby further weakening the Mohegan and Pequot nations.

Uncas had the ability to walk in the moccasins of anyone he met and that made him a skillful leader, a quick learner and a powerful friend or enemy. He loved his people and often turned the other cheek to other tribes rather than retaliate when they became envious of the growing power and respect of the Mohegan tribe. He also showed that he genuinely liked the colonists. Uncas knew that there was no honor in killing and there was a better path than the warpath.

UNCAS AND MIANTONOMO

Uncas was indeed the embodiment of the wise, fictional sachem named Uncas, whom James Fenimore Cooper described in his book, *The Last of the Mohicans*. The success of Uncas and the Mohegan tribe led to great change in the region's power structure. With the help of the Mohegan, the English triumphed against the Dutch and the Connecticut colony was at peace. The Mohegan became the unrivalled native power during colonial times. But Uncas did not live in eighteenth-century upstate New York, and he was not the "last Mohican"—he was the first Mohegan. He was responsible for the lasting of the Mohegan as a sovereign nation. He played a major part in Bolton's history and is a symbol of the very best of our Native American heritage. His son Joshua is depicted on the Bolton town seal. Thanks in part to Uncas, the four essential virtues of Native American spirituality survived: respect for God, respect for mother earth, respect for one's fellow man and respect for individual freedom.

It is said that most Connecticut Native Americans believed in one Supreme Creator, who was known in the different tribal languages as Mundo, Kiehtan, Woonand and Cantantowit. The natives placed the dwelling of the Creator in the southwest because the wind from that quarter is the warmest that blows in Connecticut and usually brings fair weather. They also believed that the soul existed after death and that the spirits of the good would go to the house of Mundo. There they would be delivered from pain and sorrow and enjoy an afterlife similar to life on earth, only in abundance and in perfection. They believed that when the wicked would go to the door of Mundo, he would tell them to go away and they were obliged to wander alone and lost forever.

Uncas showed by his actions that he not only loved his people but also cared about his defeated enemies and even about the English settlers. When overpowered by his enemies, he either turned his other cheek to avoid conflict or he turned the tables on them. He created the sovereign Mohegan nation. And in that nation he was first in friendship, first in his word of honor and first in stability and dependability. He was a Mohegan rock. In fact, the word "sachem," as Uncas was called, means "Rock Man."

The Pequot had warred against the Narragansett and other tribes, and took their lands. Now the Narragansett sought revenge. Miantonomo, sachem of the Narragansett in Rhode Island, was still filled with hatred for the Pequot, whom he helped defeat. He became envious of the growing influence of Uncas and began to engage in numerous attacks against the Mohegan homeland of Moheganeak. The Mohegan, the Mohawk and the Narragansett had sided with the English during the Pequot War. No Native American tribes supported the Pequot, who started that war. But when the Pequot survivors had been adopted into the Mohegan tribe, the hatred that Miantonomo felt for the Pequot was unfairly transferred to Uncas and the Mohegan. The Hartford General Court on October 12, 1643, noted that the Mohegan tribe under Uncas's leadership was a critically important ally to the English. The court offered the Mohegan some English soldiers to help defend against the Narragansett raids.

This eventually led to a 1644 war known as the Battle of the Great Plains. It required a large open field east of what is now Norwich, Connecticut, where Uncas would let the great Narragansett sachem Miantonomo proudly array his overwhelming army of warriors. As it happened, it was also a place where the Mohegan bow and arrow would be effective on a very large scale. Miantonomo typically attacked with upward of seven hundred warriors. While Uncas sometimes maintained as many as five hundred warriors, they were primarily defensive and spread thinly throughout Moheganeak. Uncas usually led between one and two hundred elite warriors into battle. The Mohegan warriors were the best and brightest warriors from all the other nations because Uncas welcomed all nations, offered the greatest freedom and upheld Native American traditions and virtues. The Mohegan were greatly outnumbered by the Narragansett, but Uncas had a plan. Uncas would ask Miantonomo to fight him single-handedly in mortal combat in the open field. He told his warriors that when Miantonomo refused to fight him, Uncas would drop to the ground and that would be the signal for the Mohegan warriors to fire all their arrows at the Narragansett warriors.

When Uncas fell to the ground, the Narragansett were startled and confused. Volleys of arrows struck the Narragansett but carefully missed Uncas and Miantonomo. The plan worked and most of the Narragansett warriors were finished off within a minute. Then the Mohegan attacked in hand-to-hand combat.

Miantonomo ran for his life, and was run down by the Mohegan warrior Tantaquidgeon and brought back to Uncas. Then the mighty Mohegan sachem, Uncas, with a great number of his bravest warriors and wisest and most trusted advisors (sagamores), brought Miantonomo through Bolton to the Colonial Commissioners in the Hartford colony.

Fearful of continual agitation among the native tribes, the New England colonies had established a regional group (Commission of the United Colonies) to deal with relations with the tribes, as well as trade and other issues. These commissioners decided to hand Miantonomo back to be executed in Mohegan lands by his captor, Uncas, thus avoiding any direct conflict between the Narragansett and English. Subsequently, Miantonomo was slain quickly by Uncas's brother Wawequa when they arrived at Bolton Notch. The body of wicked Miantonomo, with a hatchet buried in the back of his head, was never found, and it is said that his spirit still wanders alone and lost along the Mohegan trails through Bolton.

Uncas Helps Tontonimo

By working with the colonists, Uncas became a friend and advisor valued for his wisdom and peacekeeping ability. This gave Uncas the sovereignty and authority to manage many Indian affairs. Gradually, the Mohawk from New York relinquished their peacekeeping roles in Connecticut to Uncas.

The Nowashe were a tribe that occupied an area that is now part of Glastonbury and were the neighbors of the Podunk, who occupied what is now East Hartford and Manchester. A few Mohawk came from the Hudson valley to the Connecticut valley every two years to collect a small tribute as recognition for keeping tribal peace. One year, the Nowashe refused to pay the small tribute because they said they were not fat from the corn grown by women in the fields, nor were they foolish like their neighbors. They said they were strong hunters and built their fort on high ground. Their enemies would be weakened climbing before they could reach their fort and fight. They said they no longer needed or wanted the Mohawk or the Mohegan as peacekeepers in Connecticut.

A year passed and the surrounding tribes began to wonder if they, too, should refuse to pay tribute to the Mohawk for enforcing the tribal peace. The Mohawk suddenly came to Connecticut unannounced and borrowed many canoes from the river tribes. The main force waited upstream on the west side of the river and prepared for war, while a small advance guard of Mohawk walked inland and then downstream before they crossed the river at night in canoes and landed near where the Podunk and Nowashe lands met at the Connecticut River. The small Mohawk advance guard were seen that night destroying a teepee and crops near the Nowashe fort and left on the same trail leading back up the other side of the Connecticut River.

The Nowashe knew they could crush the few Mohawk warriors, so they dispatched most of their best warriors to track and kill them. But the trail ended far north at the river, and the Nowashe trackers could see that a large Mohawk force had camped there the previous night. The Mohawk had left and canoed down river to the Nowashe camp, and smoke could be seen rising as the Nowashe fort was overrun and burned to the ground. The Nowashe warriors who had tracked the Mohawk ran all the way back to their fort. The fastest arrived first and the slowest came much later—all slaughtered by the Mohawk, who held the high ground.

The Mohawk destroyed the Nowashe tribe except for a few who fled or who were not found. The Podunk and the Mohegan adopted the few survivors. Those survivors told all who would listen of the ferocity of the Mohawk and put fear in the hearts of all the tribes along the river.

Not long after that attack, Uncas and Tontonimo, the Podunk sachem, shared a difficult problem. A Podunk warrior named Weasseapano murdered a Mohegan sagamore living near Mattabesett. Sagamores were very wise warriors who were often subchiefs and councilors to the sachem. The murderer had become instantly popular for the daring deed, and was now undermining the authority of Tontonimo. It was unavoidable that Tontonimo had to refuse to surrender the murderer to save face so that the problem could be raised to higher authorities. When the dispute was submitted to the English, Tontonimo then agreed to surrender the murderer. However, Weasseapano had so many warrior friends that Tontonimo still could not surrender him. Now the renegades were defying Uncas and the English. The English decided that they would not trouble themselves further with the quarrel. They made Uncas understand that he and Tontonimo could solve the problem however they pleased. Uncas realized that Weasseapano was becoming the leader of the renegades who threatened Tontonimo's leadership and tribal peace. Somehow he had to strengthen Tontonimo and discredit the murderer Weasseapano.

Uncas assembled a war party to take Weasseapano prisoner, but Uncas would not have a single warrior die to capture a murderer. The Mohegan war party marched through Bolton Notch and met the renegades near the Hockanum River. Uncas showed his disappointment that so many Podunk warriors were ignoring the Indian ways and showing so little respect for the wise sagamores. He put the burden of the consequences directly on the renegades and recognized only Tontonimo as the Podunk leader by instructing the renegades to take a message back to Tontonimo. If Tontonimo continued to shelter the murderer, Uncas would send for the Mohawk to destroy Tontonimo and the entire Podunk tribe.

There is a Mohegan saying: "It is easy to be brave from a distance." The renegades suddenly had that safe distance removed. The Nowashe survivors were again trembling and telling their stories of the horror of the Mohawk attack over and over. Weasseapano suddenly lost popularity with everyone. Tontonimo went along with the strategy and reinforced the concerns of the Podunk tribe, telling everyone who would listen that Weasseapano and the renegades had put every Podunk life in jeopardy.

A few weeks later, Uncas sent a warrior with Mohawk weapons to the Podunk lands, where he set fire to a wigwam near the fort and escaped across the river, leaving some Mohawk artifacts. In the morning, when the Podunk came out of their fort to examine the ruins and look for the trail of the destroyer, they found the weapons, which they knew by their make and ornaments must have been fashioned by the Mohawk. Believing that

Uncas had succeeded in fulfilling his threat, and blinded with terror, the Podunk people now pleaded with Tontonimo to surrender Weasseapano and ask for peace.

After sufficient pleading for forgiveness, Uncas grudgingly granted peace, and from that time until King Philip's War in 1675, the Podunk remained a good tribal neighbor.

KING PHILIP'S WAR

King Philip's War, sometimes called Metacom's War, was a two-year armed conflict between Native Americans of present-day New England and English colonists and their Native American allies. After diseases had already decimated an estimated 90 percent of our Native American nation, colonial historian Francis Jennings estimated that King Philip's War killed nearly seven of every eight Native Americans living at the time and about half of the settlers. King Philip's War was proportionately one of the bloodiest and costliest in the history of America. But so long as the Mohegan had enough warriors to form a war party, Connecticut had a formidable security force and was largely immune from the raids that terrorized the rest of New England.

The colonists committed the same horrific acts in the Indian Wars as they saw Metacomet doing to settlers. So horrific were the murders, mutilations and torture of the victims that the minds of Americans almost completely blocked it out.

The Mohegan alliance with the English held while other Native American tribes chose neutrality or joined the most violent tribes in cruel attacks on isolated colonial families. Outlying towns like Simsbury, Connecticut, were abandoned and were burned to the ground by marauding war parties.

Metacomet was fatally shot by Indian John Alderman on August 12, 1676, in Bristol, Rhode Island. His wife and eight-year-old son were sold as slaves in Bermuda, while his head was mounted on a pike at the entrance to Fort Plymouth, where it remained for over two decades. His body was quartered and hung on trees. John Alderman was given one of Metacomet's hands to keep as a souvenir. These are only the things mild enough to mention here. With the exception of the Mohegan and Connecticut colonists, the depth of the depravity exhibited on both sides was so great that it is still hidden deep in the American subconscious. Connecticut was largely free from attack but provided Mohegan warriors and Connecticut soldiers to help the other colonies.

Most of the Podunk and other tribal warriors who joined Metacomet were never seen again. At the end of this war, the Mohegan tribe was the only significant tribe remaining in southern New England. The Mohegan allowed the defeated Mattabesic, Nipmuc and Narragansett to settle among them. The remnants of the Podunk and other smaller tribes were scattered and their lands were taken by the courts. That is when Podunk Indian princess Wunee Hagar was taken in as a maid in Windsor.

NATIVE AMERICANS IN THE AMERICAN REVOLUTION

Through trade and common defense, the Mohegan tribe incorporated English cultural patterns in order to survive. Yet the Mohegan maintained their sovereignty and to this day share their culture with their friends and neighbors. They still conduct the Green Corn Dance Festival of the eastern tribes every September. American Indian spiritual dance tradition survived because it is woven into the fabric of the culture so that it cannot be unraveled. The Green Corn Dance remains an important tradition, as well as the new fire in the center of dances. The new fire is the symbol of atonement for wandering from the ways of the Supreme Being, Mundo.

Native Americans held a powwow in Bolton for the bicentennial celebration of the founding of Bolton. Mary Gleason Sumner is the third person to the left of the leader. The Sumner family made a fortune and then gave it away as the largest endowment (inflation adjusted) ever to the Wadsworth Atheneum in Hartford.

When sachem Ben Uncas died in 1769, the remainder of the Mohegan homeland was assigned the protection of the family of John Mason. The Mason family succumbed to pressure in 1774 and surrendered the deed to the remaining Mohegan lands to the government of Connecticut. That ultimately made the people of Connecticut responsible for the land and morally obliged to the Mohegan. Uncas was a role model for the survival of Native Americans in a clash of cultures in the New World.

What, then, was the great difference between the Europeans and the Native Americans? It seems that the Native American tribes painted their faces to hide their humanity and appear more savage. The European tribes, on the other hand, powdered their faces and wigs to mask their savagery. The Europeans' unnatural cleanliness hid the fact that they carried the diseases that decimated the Native American tribes. And during all that time, the dying off of our Native Americans was blamed on their own customs, behavior and hygiene.

By the time of the American Revolution in 1776, only about two hundred Mohegan lived in Connecticut. Patrick M'Robert described the ancient inhabitants of America in his letters in 1774:

> *These are tall, nimble, well-made people; many of them about six feet high, with long black hair, their complexion a little tawny, or Native American-colored; their eyes black and piercing, their features good, especially the women.*
>
> *I believe the Native Americans are naturally good-natured, and obliging, when they are not ill used; but when, by bad treatment, they are obliged to take up the hatchet, they are a cruel enemy indeed. They are docile and tractable, and learn any thing fast that they wish to acquire.*

Generals Washington and Rochambeau were both warriors, and they formed alliances with our Native American nations. Washington was one of the first warriors of European descent who adopted some of the battle tactics of Native Americans. The Americans had learned from their Native American allies that it was preferable to fire from behind trees and stone walls. The aristocracy was particularly disturbed by the fact that the Americans shot at British officers. Such behavior was considered very ungentlemanly.

Many of our Native Americans, particularly the Mohegan, played an important role in bringing peace and prosperity as rangers and warriors alongside New England colonists, and later bravely serving in the Continental army of General George Washington during the Revolutionary War. The migration of many Mohegan back into New York and their mingling with other tribes helped spread the wisdom of Uncas. That wisdom was heard in the voices of many tribal leaders during the American Revolution. The newly developing American nation actively sought the help of Native Americans.

On Saturday, July 1, 1775, the journals of the Continental Congress record: "On motion, Resolved, That...the colonies ought to avail themselves of an Alliance with such Native American Nations as will enter into the same."

On August 16, 1775, Swashon, an Abenaki Chief whose thinking was similar to the Mohegan, addressed the Massachusetts House of Representatives: "As our Ancestors gave this country to you, we would not have you destroyed by England; but are ready to afford you our assistance."

Letters of General George Washington and the memoirs and diaries of the French officers show the importance of the military service and loyalty of Native Americans during this crucial period in U.S. history. Native Americans are identified with the Washington-Rochambeau Revolutionary Route and are part of the trail's heritage.

The low point for humanity occurred each time the battle lines were drawn between the native and European tribes. It was then that the tyranny of greed, oppression and cruelty reigned, regardless of the color or language. Each group, in turn, was a destroyer of its own kind, as well as the destroyer of the others. The American Revolution was a revolution in human ideals that culminated with the Declaration of Independence. At that point, the revolution was over and the war that followed was about persisting and lasting longer than the occupying British army and Tories.

During the American Revolution, most of the Native American nation and the colonists supported independence from Britain. The battle lines were drawn across each heart and mind. The battle was within us rather than between us. It was a high point for humanity because every heart had the same color and spoke the same language of hope, love and generosity. Each heart shared common truths and the same needs for dignity and respect. And every heart showed the capacity for tolerance and compassion toward strangers. When the Native Americans and colonists united in the American Revolution, a great step was taken toward replacing the tyranny of oppression and greed with liberty and the fullness of human potential.

Initially, the Mohegan and Pequot tried to cope with the Europeans in very different ways, yet their ultimate fates were quite similar. Uncas had saved the Pequot from slavery and certain death, and brought them into peaceful coexistence with the English. Thus the Pequot, along with the Mohegan, avoided the slaughter of their people in King Philip's War and other Indian wars. By following the ways learned from Uncas, both tribes remained Indian nations and ultimately regained autonomy. This was in large part due to the perseverance of the Native American women, who maintained their living culture. The Pequot regained nationhood first and then helped their brothers, the Mohegan, gain theirs. Today both tribes are proud, prosperous nations within the United States.

Part II

Promiscuous Bolton

A town is defined not by its geography but by the character and spirit of its people. As towns go, Bolton was born innocent and curious. Bolton went through its first century as a town meeting people who were doing great things, reinventing government and turning the world upside down. Sometimes it is necessary to turn things upside down to get them right side up. Sometimes, in order to do something never done before, you have to be naïve enough not to believe it can't be done that way. And sometimes, when you harbor trust, it is met with honor.

And so it was that early Bolton collected great and humorous stories of innocence, youthfulness, honor and love.

THE SETTLING OF BOLTON

Aquay! Ukiug Mohiksinug, Ukiug Unkasug, Wigwomun! Abux Wigun.
Greetings! To the Land of the Mohegan, the Land of Uncas, Welcome! May you live
happily.

—Mohegan language

It was the memory of the noble nature of the great and honorable sachems like Uncas that eventually opened the hearts of Americans. When Uncas touched pen to paper, he left his mark as a representation of himself and some of his most important beliefs. In the most prominent of these marks he placed a heart at the center, with something like a pen piercing the heart. Beneath his heart was his pipe, a gesture of friendship, honor, commitment and good will toward the nonnative people purchasing the ancient tribal lands.

When Uncas gave his word, he regarded it as a sacred trust with all peoples. He was faithful in the very best sense, honorable to his word, with that faith passed on peacefully by the Mohegan tribe through the generations. Frequently, when Uncas signed documents in which he parted with Mohegan tribal land, his mark indicated that his heart bled. That was difficult for him, so he eventually shared control of Moheganeck with his sons—Oneka the eldest son and successor, and Attanawoed. Attanawoed quickly learned the English ways. He chose a second name, Joshua, and he is depicted on the town seal of Bolton.

The oldest document on record relating to the transfer of land in Bolton is a grant by the Connecticut General Court to Captain Thomas Bull for services in the Indian Wars, bearing the date May 8, 1673. He received two hundred acres in former Podunk lands. A year later, Joshua, son of Uncas, conveyed to Major John Talcott three hundred acres of land, the more northerly and westerly half of which contained a large, boggy meadow in what is now part of Bolton. It was recorded in Hartford in 1675 (Col. Rec. Lands, iv. 334).

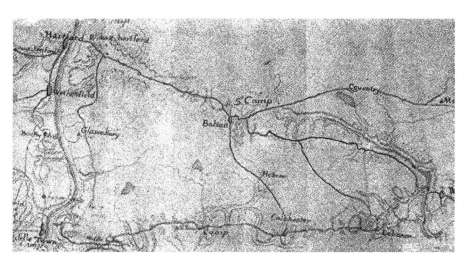

The dusty Revolutionary War pocket map carried by Continental army officers shows that Bolton was an important station on the Revolutionary Road. Bolton remained the meeting point of roads leading from the east into the Connecticut valley. Bolton was just beyond the reach of tyranny and tax agents—a town where patriots, traders, free men and commerce could move unmolested in 1776.

Bolton covers an area along the extreme western edge of the rolling eastern Connecticut upland, overlooking the Connecticut River valley to the west. It was the eastern gateway into the Connecticut valley, first used by Native Americans, and then used for the first colonial settlements in central Connecticut. This is clearly seen on the pocket map and the map of native trails (pages 36 and 18, respectively). By 1776, the colonial roads—including the Boston Post Road, the Providence Post Road and the colonial roads to Windham, Norwich, Hebron, Colchester and Lebanon—all met near Bolton Center, and left as a single road to Hartford.

The first recorded settler was Jabez Loomis in 1718, followed by Francis Smith, Stephen Bishop, Jonathan Hubbard, John Bissell and others. Bolton was part of the township of Hartford until 1720, and known as Hartford Mountains or Hanover. On October 9, 1720, the following men submitted a petition to the General Court asking for town privileges: Cullott Olcott, John Bissell, Stephen Bishop, Abiel Shaylor, Timothy Olcott, Joseph Pomeroy, Nathanial Allis, Edward Rose, John Clark, Charles Loomis, Samuel Bump, Daniel Dartt, John Church, Thomas Marshall and Samuel Raymond. Jabez Loomis of Windsor, Connecticut, recorded the first deed in 1718, found on the first page of the first volume of the Bolton Land Records. The petition was granted, and the tract of fifty one-hundred-acre lots was named Bolton by the colonial government. It is not clear why that name was chosen, but in those days it was common to name towns after the English town from which one of the head families had emigrated. By 1756, there were 751 whites, 11 blacks and 1 Native American living in Bolton.

The provision for the settlement of Bolton included a lot for the residence of a minister. The Bolton minister's lot, now called Bolton Heritage Farm, abutted the town green. Both the green and the farm were for public use during the American Revolution. Troops and weary travelers could sleep unmolested in the grass. The minister's lot had a round stone pen where stray animals were placed so that the rightful owners could find them and take them home after Sunday church. The town meetinghouse served as the church. Bolton passed a law that required every male inhabitant over sixteen years of age to work for two days each year for three years to help clear, fence and maintain that farm.

Bolton's First Ministers

The great institutions of American learning started as universities for turning out colonial pastors. Both Harvard and Yale were originally schools of divinity. Yale provided many of the pastors for Connecticut, and in 1723, when Bolton was large enough to afford a minister (seventeen active members), a young man named Jonathan Edwards came to Bolton and preached his first sermon. The congregation saw that the young man was well spoken. On May 27, 1723, the Bolton Ecclesiastical Society called him to settle as the pastor of Bolton. Jonathan replied:

> *I assure you that I have a great esteem of and affection to the people of your town, so far as I am acquainted with them, and should count it as a smile of Providence upon me if ever I should be settled among such a people as your society seems to present to me to be.*

We have in our town records an entry dated November 11, 1723, in Jonathan Edwards's handwriting:

> *November 11 1723*
> *Upon the terms that are here recorded, I do consent to be the settled pastor of this town of Bolton.*
> > *Jonathan Edwards.*

The Bolton church was not yet organized, the meetinghouse was still under construction and there was no parsonage ready for the settled pastor. That was no problem for twenty-year-old Jonathan Edwards because he could stay with his family, who lived nearby in East Windsor. So the man who was later to become one of the most celebrated writers and speakers in colonial America accepted the offer of the Town of Bolton to be the first called pastor of Bolton. However, he was not the first Bolton Congregational Church pastor, because the Bolton Congregational Church was not formed until the May 1725 session of the General Court. Reverend Edwards had accepted the call with the reservation that he would be leaving to take the next teaching vacancy at Yale. Six months later, his appointment as tutor (professor) at Yale College came through. Reverend Jonathan Edwards then recommended that his good friend Thomas White be called, and on October 25, 1725, after the Bolton Congregational Church had organized, Reverend Thomas White became Bolton Congregational Church's first pastor. He remained pastor for thirty-seven years and is buried in Bolton Center Cemetery.

Jonathan Edwards in Bolton and in Love

Jonathan Edwards (October 5, 1703–March 22, 1758) is considered New England's finest mind from the period before the American Revolution known as the Great Awakening. He spoke eloquently about what he called "the pursuit of happiness" and "the common good," ideas that became part of the Declaration of Independence and American ethics: "Some, although they love their own happiness, do not place that happiness in their own confined good, or in that good which is limited to themselves but more in the common good."

Born in East Windsor, Connecticut, just three years before Benjamin Franklin, Edwards showed precocious talent and read Newton and Locke far in advance of others in the colonies. Just before his thirteenth birthday, he went off to Yale College, where he graduated as class valedictorian with all honors at age seventeen. He then helped in a small congregation in New York City for a brief time. He returned to Connecticut by boat in April 1723. At a Bolton town meeting on May 27, 1723, it was voted to call Reverend Jonathan Edwards, age twenty, to become the first pastor in Bolton. Reverend Edwards spent the summer with his parents in East Windsor and visited Bolton, then a small crossroads hamlet, in June 1723, as he walked to Boston. In his diary, he describes his spiritual reconciliation and epiphany in Bolton at that time:

> [T]*here came into my soul, and was as it were diffused through it, a sense of the glory of the Divine Being; a new sense, quite different from any thing I ever experienced before. I thought with myself, how excellent a Being that was, and how happy I should be, if I might enjoy that God, and be rapt up to him in heaven, and be as it were swallowed up in him for ever!*

Jonathan Edwards had been troubled since childhood by the thought that God might reject people who, through no fault of their own, had not come to know Christ. Edwards's epiphany resolved his concern—people who had never heard the particular name of Christ might be swallowed up in God as well. His diary and notes have revealed an Edwards very different from the stern philosopher presented to earlier generations. Something changed in Edwards that summer:

> *The appearance of every thing was altered. God's excellency, his wisdom, his purity and love, seemed to appear in every thing; in the sun, moon, and stars; in the clouds, and blue sky, in the grass, flowers, trees; in the water,*

and all nature. I spent most of my time in thinking of divine things, often walking alone in the woods, and solitary places, for meditation, soliloquy, and prayer, and converse with God.

Reverend Edwards tried to put God first in everything he did. However, as he studied for his Master of Arts, he wrote the following note in the margins of one of his textbooks. Clearly he had fallen in love with a girl he had not yet even met:

They say there is a young lady in New Haven who is beloved of that Great Being who made and rules the world, and that there are certain seasons in which this Great Being, in some way or other invisible, comes to her and fills her mind with exceeding sweet delight, and that she hardly cares for any thing, except to meditate on Him. She is of a wonderful sweetness, calmness and universal benevolence of mind; specially after this great God has manifested Himself to her Mind. She will sometimes go about from place to place, singing sweetly; and seems to be always full of joy and pleasure; and no one knows for what. She loves to be alone, walking in the fields and groves, and seems to have some one invisible always conversing with her.

Jonathan Edwards wrote that he had his epiphany while walking in the fields of Bolton.

Jonathan Edwards's wife, Sarah Edwards, circa 1733. Jonathan wrote about Sarah in his Yale textbooks in 1723, just before he accepted the call to be Bolton's minister. He left Bolton in 1724 to teach at Yale and to be near Sarah.

He met the girl, Sarah, for the first time in New Haven that September after passing his exams with flying colors. Edwards was twenty years old, and Sarah was then thirteen years old. She was the daughter of James Pierrepont, the minister of the New Haven church and one of the founders of Yale. One of her great-grandfathers was Thomas Hooker, who brought the first settlers of Hartford, Connecticut. Another great-grandfather was the first mayor of New York City. When the tall, gawky, intense and studious Edwards first met Sarah, she was frightened by him, but then she quickly fell in love. Edwards made an awkward beau, looking on as Sarah shined in social situations. Edwards returned and accepted the position as pastor in Bolton on November 11, 1723, but could hardly wait for the position at Yale to open. Within two weeks of receiving the Yale offer in May 1724, he left Bolton and was on his way to New Haven, where he assumed the position of senior tutor at Yale in June 1724.

The usually focused Edwards later felt guilty for his very perplexing and deeply distracting love for Sarah, but that did not diminish this love. He wrote, "After I went to New Haven, I sunk in religion; my mind being diverted from my eager pursuits after holiness, by some affairs, that greatly perplexed and distracted my thoughts."

On July 28, 1727, in the year of his ordination, Edwards married Sarah Pierrepont (then age seventeen) in New Haven. She brought to him strength and a never-failing sweetness for the next thirty years. The real Jonathan Edwards was a tender husband, an affectionate father and a human soul quite unlike the image of him as a stern preacher. Edwards described his happy marriage to Sarah as their uncommon union bonded to one another and also bonded to the living God. He fathered eleven children.

In 1739, Edwards published his *Personal Narrative*, which specifically linked his epiphany and reconciliation to God to his experience in the fields of Bolton in the summer of 1723. It no doubt occurred in the fields of the Minister's Farm that was then being prepared and that is now Bolton Heritage Farm. He makes it clear that this blissful period lasted for the entire duration that he was pastor in Bolton:

> *It was a comfort to think of that state, where there is fullness of joy; where reigns heavenly, calm, and delightful love, without alloy; where there are continually the dearest expressions of this love; where is the enjoyment of the persons loved, without ever parting; where those persons who appear so lovely in this world, will really be inexpressibly more lovely, and full of love to us. I continued much in the same frame, in the general, as when at New York, till I went to New Haven, as Tutor of the College: particularly, once at Bolton, on a journey from Boston, while walking out alone in the fields.*

Jonathan Edwards is recognized as America's most profound and original philosophical theologian. His work was very broad in scope, but most people, if they know Edwards at all, still think of him as a fiery preacher of "Sinners in the Hands of an Angry God." Students are surprised when they learn that Edwards seldom raised his voice when preaching.

Edwards also played a role in the Enlightenment. He was a genius who had the capacity and imagination to hold onto traditional truths yet reconcile and restate them in the language of the learned world around him. He possessed an insatiable curiosity, not just about religion but about life, too. Edwards's calm oratory ignited spiritual ardor in the heart, working through the mind. He conceived of God as a being who wants or even needs to communicate his divine love intimately to us, his creation. He regarded nature with reverence and as a source of divine inspiration.

Jonathan Edwards lived during a time of difficult transition, from the Colonial to the Revolutionary periods. In 1758, he became the third president of Princeton University. When an experimental smallpox vaccine was to be tested on Princeton students, Jonathan Edwards insisted that it be tested on him first to make sure it was safe. That was the cause of his death—softness of the heart.

PROMISCUOUS SINGING IN BOLTON

A major controversy was raging when the church was established in Bolton and Reverend Thomas White became the first church pastor. The controversy illustrates not only how much times have changed, but also the power of words in triggering our imaginations.

It was John Hammet who published an essay in 1739, condemning promiscuous singing, titled, "Promiscuous Singing No Divine Institution":

> *Having neither Precedent nor Precept to support it, either from the Musical Institution of David, or from the Gospel Dispensation. Therefore it ought to be exploded, as being a humane Invention, tending rather to gratify the carnal.*

The reaction of some church congregations to promiscuous singing was described by Cotton Mather in a letter to Thomas Hollis in 1723:

> *Numbers of Elder and Angry People bore zealous Testimonies against these wicked Innovations, and this bringing in of Popery. Their zeal transported some of them so far that they would not only use the most opprobrious terms and call the Singing of these Christians a worshipping of the Devil, but they also would run out of the Meeting house at the Beginning of the Exercise.*

Promiscuous singing was not always done with one's spouse. Sometimes men did it together in the back pews. Sometimes it was done by men and women in front of their children. Harmonious promiscuous singing was considered such an abomination unto God, and such a departure from the straight and narrow, that it was debated in Hartford.

Nathaniel Chauncy logically stated the case before the General Association at Hartford, Connecticut, in 1727—that it was known that there was a "sure and certain Rule" for singing and further that there were ill effects caused by the neglect of this rule:

In case there be various Rules, they must lead to differing Ends to be sure, differing, in proportion to the difference there is in the Rules or Means. And this shews [sic] it can't be a matter of indifference how we Sing: Because that various Rules, or various Means lead to various Ends.

From the earliest settlements of the Plymouth and Massachusetts Bay Colonies, singing in churches had been performed without accompanying music and frequently used lining-out. Lining-out consisted of someone leading by singing each line, which the congregation in turn repeated. That practice was the solution to the early problems of illiteracy and a shortage of hymnbooks. The tunes were personalized according to the leader's interpretation and abilities. The hymns gradually became unrecognizable from church to church. In the 1720s, when Bolton was founded, lining-out was still in use in most churches in New England, even though there were then plenty of hymnbooks available and literacy was perhaps even higher than it is today.

But there were still some people who remembered that singing could touch the heart and be beautiful and harmonious, all at the same time. Just as the opponents of regular harmonious singing exaggerated and called it "promiscuous singing," the advocates of instituting harmonious singing argued that the awful sound of lining-out could induce spontaneous miscarriages, as described by James Franklin, writing for the *New-England Courant*, on February 17 and 24, in 1724:

I am credibly inform'd, that a certain Gentlewoman miscarry'd at the ungrateful and yelling Noise of a Deacon in reading the first Line of a Psalm: and methinks if there were no other Argument against this Practice (unless there were an absolute necessity for it) the Consideration of its being a Procurer of Abortion, might prevail with us to lay it aside.

The debate of such carnal pleasures as regular harmonious singing (promiscuous singing) versus line singing (spontaneous miscarriage-inducing singing) was so contentious that it was left up to each congregation to decide. Harmonious singing was the choice of Reverend Thomas White in Bolton from the start, because it was taught at Yale. Serious debate over whether choirs, musical instruments or pipe organs would be allowed broke out in the latter part of the 1700s when Dr. George Colton was pastor. Yet even greater controversies arose in Bolton, such as the use of the wicked invention of the pernicious and perfidious bouncing rubber ball, which induced idleness, startled cattle and horses and broke numerous windows. Democracy and tolerance prevailed in the end.

So Cold, the Rich Had to Beg

During the last million years, as the earth has continued to cool, ten great ice ages have come and passed. Each ice age was followed by global warming—at first the cycle melted all the ice, but as the earth has continued to cool, the earth has more recently begun to retain some polar ice throughout the cycle. Within the ice age cycle there are mini cycles. The last mini ice age ended in the mid-1800s. Bolton town clerk John Bissell gave one of the earliest weather reports in 1741. It was published for the first time in the *Hartford Times* on February 18, 1899.

The winter of 1740–41 arrived early, with October "as cold as ordinarily November is," wrote our town clerk John Bissell, and a substantial snowfall hit in mid-November. After that, two solid weeks of rain in early December severely damaged "bridges, fences, hay" and ruined "the Indian corn chambers, cribs." "Extreme cold" followed and "traveling was almost wholly suspended by reason of the extreme cold and deep snow, and God had sealed up the hand of every man." There was also a very sensible consideration: "Who can stand before His cold!!!"

In January, drifting snow soon brought an end to regular travel by highway in New England and the Middle Colonies, and the penetrating cold closed all the rivers and waterways with solid ice. One man made a two-hundred-mile trip by sleigh over the frozen sound from Cape Cod to New York City. The extreme cold was not confined to the Northeast. That year the York River in Virginia froze solid enough to cross. "Notwithstanding the settling of the snow, the snow on the sixth day of March was three foot deep," wrote Bissell. "The weather continued cold and the snow wasted but slowly, so that there was considerable quantity of snow the middle of April." The Connecticut River was still frozen solid enough to be crossed on the first of April.

This unparalleled cold weather produced a story of extraordinary survival. "At Guilford, a Sheep was in the winter buried in a storm of snow and lay there ten weeks and three days and came out alive," reported Bissell.

Shortages arose, "by reason of which scarcity a great number of cattle and horses died, and near half the sheep, and about two thirds of the goats," wrote Bissell.

Exceeding scarcity followed, partly by reason of the abundance of Indian corn being ruined by the long rains in December, and partly by people giving their corn to their creatures to save their lives. We suppose the ensuing summer was the greatest scarcity as ever the English felt since the first settlement of this government. Indian corn rose in the price from ten to

Bolton Town Clerks
Francis Smith 1720. 1721
John Bissell 1722 - 1752
Thomas Pitkin 1753 - 1765
Capt. Benjamin Talcott 1766 - 1779 1780 82+8
Saul Alvord 1775 from 1789 to 1793 1795 to 1800
from 1802 to 1805, Saul Alvord Junr 2
Elijah White 1781 1788
Oliver King 1748. 1794. 1799. 7801. 1816. 1807
Saul Alvord Jr 1808. 1809. 1838 to 1842
Elijah White 1810. 1811
Daniel Lord 1812 to 1815
Manton Hammond 1815 to 1833
George Clinton White 1833 to 1836
Samuel Ruggles 1837
Luther Talcott 1842 to 1847
William Kenny 1848
Elisha K Williams 1849 to 1864
George G Sumner 1865. 1866
Sherman P Sumner 1867 to 1871 1874 to 1888
Horace Witherell 1882
Dr Charles F Sumner 1889
W B Williams 1890
Charles F Sumner Junr 1891 to 1895
J. White Sumner from Jan 1, 1895 to June 15, 1953
(date of death)
David C. Toomey June 21, 1933 to May 10, 1962
Olive H. Toomey August 1, 1962 to August 1, 1972
(date of death)
Catherine T. Leiner August 1, 1972 to July 1, 1993
Susan M. DePold July 1, 1993 to

John Bissell was Bolton's second town clerk and served from 1722 until 1752. He gave his famous freezing weather report in 1741. The town clerk was an elected position for most of Bolton's history. The current town clerk was elected and then became the first to be appointed by the board of selectmen.

twenty shillings, and what was commonly sold for twenty shillings, till at last all buying and selling utterly ceased. Money was no temptation, and men of good estates who had money was [sic] found to put themselves into the quality of beggars, and beg sometimes two quarts at a place, to relieve the distresses of their poor families.

As dreadful as the winter of 1740–41 had been, the winter of 1779–80 was the worst ever recorded from Maine to Georgia. It was the infamous winter in Valley Forge, where the Continental army left bloody footprints in the snow. The next summer, the French army arrived to support the American Revolution and the Duc de Lauzun, a colonel whose legion of Hussars was assigned to winter in nearby Lebanon, Connecticut, compared it to being sent to Siberia.

Although snow first fell in the Northeast in early November 1779, winter did not begin in earnest until the middle of December, when a series of invading Arctic air masses dominated the weather scene for the next thirteen weeks. Farther south it was possible to walk across the firmly frozen Chesapeake Bay in Maryland and the Albemarle Sound in North Carolina. Harbors in Virginia froze like stone. Sleighs traveled the ice from Staten Island to Manhattan Island, and for a time people traversed the sound from Connecticut to Long Island.

The frigid air was soon accompanied by an unprecedented series of three major nor'easters that ravaged the entire coastal plain from Virginia northward and lasted until the winter breakup in mid-March.

Accounts varied, but by mid-January, the standing snow was reportedly four feet deep in Connecticut, with massive drifts. Frozen ports and snow-clogged roads paralyzed daily activity. Forced to winter in New London when his ship got stuck in the ice of the Thames River, Captain Jean-Francois Landolphe recorded in his diary that "so much snow fell over a three-day period that it rose above the windows of the second story, in such manner that daylight could not penetrate. I had never seen anything like it."

But then the weather worsened and the temperature plunged. The *Connecticut Courant* reported that readings of a new device called a "thermometer" were below zero on eleven days, including a low of twenty-two degrees below zero in Hartford on January 29, 1780.

"To set up communications with my neighbors across the street I had a vaulted passage dug beneath the snow," Landolphe continued. "The cold set in again with an extraordinary harshness. It made us all numb."

The fireplace in the Ruggles' house was representative of the norm in colonial Bolton. Colonial homes were chilly even though the massive stone chimney radiated heat well after the flames died down. It was said that a servant once fell into one of these dangerous hearths. Her tombstone read, "Well done, good and faithful servant."

Newspapers found themselves in a news blackout as the stagecoaches stopped running. On January 11, the *Connecticut Courant* informed its readers, "The late violent Snow Storms have prevented the Posts from performing their usual stages; in consequence of which we have received no papers from the Eastward or Westward later than the 23d of December."

Three major snowstorms closed all main roads in New England for the duration of the winter, with the exception of the Boston Post Road through Bolton, which was broken out and became passable by January 20. Side roads generally were impassable until the March thaw. In New London, Captain Landolphe's men used saws to cut a path in the frozen river to open water. After two days of cutting, their ship was finally freed on May 10, 1780.

The weather forecast for Bolton is thirty-five thousand years of global warming, followed by the start of the next ice age.

DR. COLTON OF BOLTON

The next pastor in Bolton, the Reverend George Colton, served forty-nine years, including the period of the American Revolution. Reverend Colton stood six feet eight inches tall, had steel-blue eyes and wore a large wig. At one service, a little girl saw Reverend Colton coming down the aisle wearing his wig and shouted in excitement, "Oh, mother, here comes a man with a sheep on his head!" His face was stern, and at least one man in town admitted that, as a boy, he would jump behind the nearest stone wall and hide when the minister swung down his road in Bolton.

The Reverend Dr. George Colton was educated at Yale, ordained in 1763 and settled in Bolton as our town's minister on the property now known as the Bolton Heritage Farm. He was well respected and known for his wisdom and good humor. At his home, he entertained President Styles of Yale University, General George Washington, several French and Continental army officers and had General Rochambeau as an overnight guest twice. The French expeditionary army camped on his fields. French officers noted in their diaries that on his head he wore a high, frizzy, blue-white wig that made him appear even taller than he was. Dr. Colton towered over everyone and was known as "the High Priest of Bolton."

On March 4, 1781, General Washington stopped and had lunch with the Coltons as Washington was traveling to Newport to talk with General Rochambeau. Washington and Colton must have had an intimate conversation, because Washington wrote that George Colton had no children. It was a concern both men shared—Washington, the father of America, also fathered no children.

Several German states bordering France provided half of the French troops in America. In those times, soldiers could be away from home for three or four years. Several of the soldiers therefore paid to have their families follow them in the long stream of camp followers. Aristocrats like Lafayette received an annual income at that time that was approximately fifty thousand times greater than the average French soldier. Having no children of their own, the Coltons felt sorry for some of the children of the French and German soldiers who camped on their fields during Rochambeau's march to Yorktown. Colton explained his situation to one of the soldiers and raised the question of adoption, offering a good stable home. The soldier hesitated, so Reverend Colton offered to compensate him for his troubles. The generous amount of money he offered was about ten years' salary for the soldier. The soldier declined the offer, and the news spread through the army all the way to the Paris newspapers, where Reverend Colton's offer and the high honor and dignity of the soldier made the headlines.

Reverend George Colton refused to have his portrait painted, calling it a display of pure vanity. However, while portrait artist Ralph Earl was living in Bolton, someone sketched Reverend Colton during a service and then painted a rather severe visage of him. This is a less austere copy of the original, which was last known to be in the possession of the Connecticut Historical Society.

In another story, there was someone living in Gay City Hollow that did impersonations of Dr. Colton. Gay City was a small hamlet on the border of Bolton and Andover on West Street, settled by a hardworking, hard-drinking religious sect. So one day, Reverend Colton took off his church attire, disguised himself and went to the Gay City area to mingle with the people and talk to the impersonator. Colton challenged him to see who could do a better impersonation of Colton. Several Gay City neighbors assembled to do the judging. Dr. Colton lost the contest but he was acknowledged to be a fairly good impersonator himself. Dr. Colton, in good humor, would say, "There is no harm in imitating the righteous."

In a third story, the Reverend Dr. George Colton went to Hartford to hear a lecture by Dr. Strong of the Center Church. Dr. Strong's buoyant wit was a match for Dr. Colton's. At the opening of the lecture, the towering form of the High Priest of Bolton entered and Dr. Strong welcomed him saying, "Dr. Colton of Bolton, will you come this way and pray?" Dr. Colton replied, "Dr. Strong, you do wrong at such a time to make a rhyme." To which Dr. Strong replied, "Dr. Colton of Bolton, I plainly see that at making rhymes you are as bad as me."

Dr. Colton performed his last wedding, that of Sarah White to Samuel Williams, on March 12, 1812, and died June 27, 1812.

BUNDLING IN BOLTON

It's time to set the record straight! It's time to admit that it was we who shocked the French, and not the other way around.

When Rochambeau's French army came to fight for American independence, its soldiers sported more ribbons and petticoats than our Connecticut young ladies. The French had more formal-looking smocks for underwear than the Bolton locals wore on Sunday. They prudishly changed in their tall tents while the local young people skinny-dipped in the rivers and streams.

You can imagine how surprised and disarmed the soldiers were when our young ladies entered the privacy of their tents as they sat about in their frilly smocks. The diaries of the French officers tell those stories and more. Americans, with their vivaciousness and innocence, gave the French many shocking stories to write home about.

On October 28, 1782, General Verger wrote the following in his diary as he prepared to return through Bolton after the war was won:

> *When they visited our camp, the girls came without their mothers and entered our tents with the greatest confidence. I cannot refrain from reporting a very extraordinary custom of this charming province, which is known as "bundling."*
>
> *A stranger or a resident who frequents a house and takes a fancy to a daughter of the house may declare his love in the presence of her father and mother without their taking it amiss; if she looks with favor upon his declaration and permits him to continue his suit, he is at perfect liberty to accompany her wherever he wants without fear of reproach from her parents…Then if he is on good terms with the lady, he can propose bundling with her…*
>
> *The man may remove his coat and shoes but nothing more, and the girl takes off nothing but her kerchief. Then they lie down together on the same bed, even in the presence of the mother—and the most strict mother. If they are alone in the room and indiscreet ardor leads the man to rashness toward his Dulcinea, woe to him if the least cry escapes her, for then the entire house enters the room and beats the lover for his too great impetuosity. Regardless of appearances, it is rare that a girl takes advantage of this great freedom, which confirms the good faith of these amiable citizens.*

The culture shock of meeting such innocent, loving and trusting people was more than the French soldiers could understand. That made the French behave all the more gallantly and honorably.

Bundling was a test of the ultimate loving relationship of caring, respecting, cuddling and self-control. It occurred in the house, so the lad knew his girlfriend's parents might hear anything. It made more sense for the parents this way because they had no control over what happened in the hayloft, fields or forest. When a couple was ready for engagement, the young man might be allowed to spend the entire night in the same bed as the intended bride, especially if it was getting late and he was exhausted from working with the family that day. But strict religious beliefs prohibited certain things and restraint and maturity usually made a boy into a man by age eighteen. The solution was pure American ingenuity. The mother would often sew the lad into a large sack, with only his head sticking out, so his hands and other appendages were contained within the sack. The daughter was in control and could do as she pleased with the defenseless lad, as long as her parents, brothers and sisters were not disturbed in the adjoining rooms.

The adorable custom of bundling allowed intimacy so that parties of marriageable age could talk quietly when the heavy work of the day had been completed. The practice was usually limited to the winter and sometimes included the use of a bundling board, placed between the boy and girl.

But what about the long-term health and psychological effects of this Bolton bundling custom?

On June 22, 1781, General Clermont-Crevecour wrote the following in his diary upon traveling from Bolton to East Hartford:

> *We have seen old people here of both sexes who enjoy perfect health at a very advanced age. Their old age is gay and amiable, and not at all burdened with the infirmities that are our lot in our declining years…Foreigners are cordially received by these good people.*

No doubt these older married people kept their youthfulness and feistiness by bundling on cold Bolton winter nights. That makes at least two Bolton traditions: placing candles in windows during the Christmas season, and bundling—yes, also preferably by candlelight.

Ralph Earl and Dr. Cooley

Born in Shrewsbury, Massachusetts, on May 11, 1751, Ralph Earl was one of America's earliest landscape artists. Ralph had established himself as a portrait painter in New Haven by 1774. There he saw the portraits of John Singleton Copley, which had an enduring impact on him and inspired works such as Earl's notable full-length portrait of Roger Sherman. Earl's rough-hewn, laborious, direct approach brings inner qualities of the sitter into full relief. Earl painted Sherman in browns and blacks, looking doggedly ahead.

In 1775, working in New Haven, Earl and engraver Amos Doolittle visited the recent battle scenes at Lexington and Concord. Earl's four painted battle pictures, engraved by Doolittle, were among the earliest Revolutionary War scenes done in America. The forms are sharply drawn, with little modeling, and take on the look of flat paper cutouts.

Earl's father was a colonel in the Continental army, but Earl, refusing to fight against the king's troops and fearing for his safety, fled to England in 1778, where he remained for seven years. William Dunlap's history of American art, published in 1834, observed that Earl prevented improvement and destroyed himself by habitual intemperance.

After his return to America, he made portraits of Timothy Dwight, Governor Caleb Strong and other prominent men. In September 1786, while living in New York City, Earl was imprisoned for failing to pay his personal debts. While in jail, he drew portraits of his visitors, friends and family of the Society for the Relief of Distressed Debtors. He was released in January 1788.

Earl then became a traveling artist in Connecticut. His colors grew brighter and his figures more supple, but his paintings still had the primitive, seventeenth-century look, which was not uncommon at that time. Traveling around New England, he painted notable citizens of the new republic, Revolutionary War heroes and everyday people in their natural surroundings. Among the best are the portrait of Daniel Boardman (1789), in which a lovely grassy landscape, with soft mists falling over the hills, stretches behind the figure. His Connecticut landscapes of the 1790s are precise and factual yet manage to catch the personality of the place.

Ralph Earl spent the last two years of his life in Bolton in the home of prominent local physician, Dr. Samuel Cooley, on South Road. There, dying from the debilitating effects of his heavy drinking, Earl received friendship, comfort and medical treatment. The Cooley family raised several notable children in their home while Ralph Earl was living there. Three sons became

While Dr. Samuel Cooley lived on South Road, he took in artist Ralph Earl as an act of charity and cared for him for the last two years of Earl's life.

Dr. Samuel Abbott Cooley, grandson of Dr. Samuel Cooley and a well-known Civil War photographer, was said to be the spitting image of his grandfather.

doctors. Dr. Samuel Abbott Cooley, grandson of Dr. Samuel Cooley and a well-known Civil War photographer, was said to be the spitting image of his grandfather.

Ralph Earl was said to have wanted to paint Reverend Colton, but Reverend Colton would have none of such vanity. Although the reverend was tall and stood in a high pulpit, children at the time said they could barely see him over the high-backed pews. It was by hiding his sketch paper behind a high pew that a congregation member managed to sketch Reverend Colton and then paint his portrait when he got home. A copy of the original painting was painted by Robert McKee in May 1879, and donated to the Bolton Congregational Church.

Two of the greatest unsolved mysteries of Bolton are what happened to the original portrait painting of Dr. Colton and who painted it. At the time of an article in the *Hartford Courant* on June 22, 1908, the original hung in Memorial Hall on Asylum Street in Hartford. It was believed to be the

Bolton Center Cemetery has a famous row of tombstones. Huddled together are the tombstones of Reverend White and Reverend Colton and the monument to artist Ralph Earl (seen in the forefront). Captain Joel White has an unusual stone table shielding his plot nearby. Locals report ghostly weather behavior and spectacular light shows when electrical storms start in Bolton Notch and pass down the valley.

property of the Connecticut Historical Society. We cannot determine who painted Colton until the original painting is found and tested by experts. The fact that Reverend Colton would not permit anyone to officially paint him does not rule out the high probability that the artist was Ralph Earl who was attending the Bolton Congregational Church when Colton was of the age depicted in the painting. The painting was in the simple, primitive style of artist Ralph Earl.

Ralph Earl's cause of death in 1801 was listed by Reverend Colton as "intemperance." His stone is located in a row with other famous early Bolton residents.

Part III

Revolutionary Bolton

Bolton is painted with Revolutionary War heritage. Amid the dabs of white houses and splotches of red barns, there are hard fields of pastel green where General Washington's deployed soldiers rested and dreamed of independence. Bolton was born on a path just beyond the reach of tyranny and its tax agents—a road where patriots, traders, commerce and free men could move unmolested in 1776. From the Redcoats' perspective, this is the route that every no-good traitor, revolutionary, smuggler and loud-mouthed rabble-rouser used to keep a safe distance from their rule of law. Every American patriot used a portion of it and it just happened to be the main street in Bolton.

OLIVER WHITE TAVERN

French maps from the Revolutionary War have the Oliver White Tavern indicated at Brandy Street, just past the Loomis House. The records indicate that Oliver White bought the land in 1741 and sold it with a house on it in 1743. It was customary to refer to houses by the names of their original owners, and when taverns sold they would keep their original name to keep the good will of the customers. In early America, taverns were not just respectable, they were a necessity. As early as 1644, the colonial records of Connecticut ordered "one sufficient inhabitant" in each town to keep an ordinary (tavern), since "strangers were straitened for want of entertainment."

The Loomis House on Brandy Street is shown in a photo taken about 1931. The Loomis family was among the original settlers of Bolton.

The Bolton taverns were made for the convenience of travelers, the comfort of our townspeople, the interchange of news and opinions, the sale of refreshments and beverages and for incidental sociability. In fact, the importance of the tavern to Bolton residents was far greater than it was to travelers. During the 1700s, when there were no office buildings, banks or post offices, taverns served all those functions. It was in taverns that Bolton lumber and quarry stone were bought and sold, new companies formed, militia inducted, stagecoaches stopped and mail distributed.

The taverns played an important role in the development of a colonial transportation network. Bolton was situated on the fastest route connecting Boston, Hartford, New York and Philadelphia. The early Bolton taverns that served stagecoaches were located on the Boston Post Road and the Providence and Hartford Roads. All three of those roads converged on Bolton Center during the Revolution and went past or very close to the Oliver White Tavern. Prior to the Revolution, it was a major smuggling route located far from the British tariff and tax collectors. During the Revolution, it was the main route in New England used to deploy and supply the Continental and

French armies. Connecticut was then the pantry of the colonies, and soon became its armory as well.

Innkeepers reflected the high public status accorded their establishments. Publicans were commonly among a town's most prominent citizens and not infrequently were deacons of the church and town meeting moderators. During the Revolutionary War, the Oliver White Tavern located on East Street (now Brandy Street) was owned by Captain Joel White and became a favorite inn of French and American officers. To this day, it has bayonet holes left by French troops in the ceiling of one of the bedrooms.

A new pastor's ordination day was almost as great a day for the tavern as for the meetinghouse. The visiting ministers who came to assist at the religious service were usually entertained at the tavern. Often an especially good beer was brewed called "ordination beer," and in Connecticut an "ordination ball" was given at the tavern—all with the sanction of the ministers.

On September 5, 1774, the town records show that Captain Joel White was the town meeting moderator. At that meeting, Bolton decided to send Captain Thomas Pitkin and Seth King to Hartford to discuss a possible boycott of British goods. That was the first step that led to American independence. During the Revolution, Captain Joel White lent £3,000 to the State of Connecticut and to the United States. He was a Bolton justice of the peace, town treasurer and a representative to the state legislature.

Captain Joel White was one of the proprietors of the Oliver White in Bolton. Bolton artist Susan Bosworth painted the house as seen in winter, when it is a Bolton custom to put candles in the windows as a sign of friendship. This was first done in 1780, when the French army landed in Newport on English territory, and the townspeople lit candles to show that the French soldiers were welcome.

If they were good hosts, publicans did their best to make patrons comfortable. There was no putting on of airs, no exclusiveness. All travelers sat at one large table. The traveler paid not for a whole room but for a place in a bed. Many of the rooms had two beds, and four complete strangers often slept in one room. After the traveler was asleep, the landlord often entered, candle in hand, with yet another stranger to share the bed till morning. It was said that anyone who objected to a stranger as a bedfellow was regarded as intolerable or unreasonably fastidious.

But the tavern wasn't for everyone. One woman traveling alone wrote of her experience at a tavern in another town:

> *Being exceedingly weary down I laid my poor carcass never more tired and found my covering as scanty as my bed was hard. Anon I heard another ruselling noise in the room—called to know the matter—Little Miss said she was making a bed for the men; who when they were in Bed complain'd their Leggs lay out of it by reason of its shortness—my poor bones complained bitterly not being used to such Lodgings, and so did the man who was with us {me}; and poor I made but one Grone which was from the time I went to bed to the time I riss which was about three in the morning setting up by the fire till light.*

It was an age of innocence, civility, respect and honor. Captain Joel White is buried in Bolton Center Cemetery and has an ancient and unique monument that resembles a large stone tavern table.

THE WASHINGTON-ROCHAMBEAU REVOLUTIONARY ROUTE

The Native American trails were the first colonial settlement routes through Bolton. The Mohegan trail was a major path, running along the Hop River, through the notch and on to Hartford. That early settlement road entered Bolton through Bailey Road, ran onto Brandy Street, past the Oliver White Tavern, turned left past what is now the Bolton Heritage Farm, then through the center of town and finally exited on Bolton Center Road. Now we call it the Washington-Rochambeau Revolutionary Route (W3R) because it became the route used by French and American troops. The earliest, detailed, hand-copied colonial pocket maps (page 36) show that the route branches farther east and south of Bolton, with one heading eastward toward Providence and the other southeast toward Norwich. Until the War of Independence, there were few intercolonial routes available because the British wanted to control trade for tax purposes and therefore discouraged the colonies from avoiding taxes by trading directly with one another. They made that the crime of smuggling. The W3R was the safe route that the Patriots used when they deployed troops. The Connecticut forces, the Continental army and Governor Trumbull himself often used the road.

We know that Bolton was a thriving town at the time of the Revolution, strategically located one day out of Hartford at the very nexus of the roads connecting Hartford with Boston, Providence, Lebanon and Norwalk. In 1776, it was on the fastest route from New York and Philadelphia to both Boston (the Middle Post Road) and Providence. When the inns were full, the town green and the present Bolton Heritage Farm were the places troops and travelers were welcome to camp.

General Rochambeau traveled on the route through Bolton six times—twice in September 1780 to and from the Hartford Conference, where he first met General Washington; twice for the strategic meeting with Washington in May 1780; and again twice leading the French army to and from Yorktown, Virginia. General Washington used it March 4, 1781, when, accompanied by Alexander Hamilton, he visited Rochambeau at Newport. The eastern entrance to Bolton from Coventry in 1781 was the muddy and stony Bailey Road, which is in an important Bolton wetlands complex. Andover did not exist at the time, and the French maps show that Camp Forty-six was considered part of Bolton at that time.

Others known to have traveled on this section of the Revolutionary Route include Lafayette, General Chastellux, General Varnum, General Henry Knox, the Duc de Lauzun, Benjamin Franklin, Nathan Hale, Private Jeremiah Greenman and several other American and French officers.

Revolutionary War maps drawn by a French engineer indicate that the Boston Post Road moved from Bailey Road, and by 1781, it entered from Coventry on Stony Road and then on Toomey Road to Bolton Center. That means all the Patriots going between Hartford and Boston on the northern route still passed through the center of Bolton until the Turnpike Era. By 1795, the Boston Turnpike was created and it bypassed the center of town and went directly through the Bolton Notch. It created Quarryville, with Notch Hollow at its center. Quarryville grew larger in population than Bolton Center during the next century. In 1916, most of the Revolutionary Road was incorporated into the new highway system as Route 6. Many abandoned or bypassed sections of the Revolutionary Road exist today—like Bailey Road, Bolton Heritage Farm and Bolton Center—that are very similar to the way they looked to the Patriots and the French in 1780 and 1782.

Bailey Road in Bolton, used by Rochambeau and American patriots, went through wetlands. By 1795, almost all traffic had moved to what is now Watrous Road. Bailey Road therefore remained a colonial road and was never upgraded to a turnpike. In 2000, it was put on the National Register of Historic Places.

EARLY BOLTON HEROES

Jonathan Birge married Pricilla Hammond on March 24, 1763, and lived on Hebron Road in Bolton. On March 15, 1775, Jonathan Birge was commissioned a captain in the Crown's army. All Americans were then subjects of the English Crown. Governor Jonathan Trumbull was the Crown's governor in Connecticut. Benjamin Franklin was the postmaster general in the American colonies. However, by 1775, loyalties were divided and many were already Americans first and Englishmen second.

Historic Tales

The Lexington Alarm of April 19, 1775, is considered the beginning of the Revolutionary War. It made instant traitors of thousands of the Crown's militia who rode out to support the people of Boston. It started with the ride of Paul Revere and the British attacks on Lexington and Concord. State records show that sixty-three men from Bolton marched on the Revolutionary Route to the relief of Massachusetts minutemen. That compares with forty-five from the much larger town of Hartford. From Bolton, Jonathan Birge and Thomas Pitkin were captains and Jared Cone and Isaac Fellows were lieutenants. The British quickly withdrew to Boston as a sea of four thousand armed militiamen swelled across the Massachusetts countryside, took the heights overlooking Boston and ignited the skies with bonfires. General Washington then positioned cannons taken from the Redcoats at Fort Ticonderoga, New York, on the heights overlooking Boston, forcing the withdrawal of the British occupying army. The thousands of armed Americans who participated in these acts were now considered traitors to the Crown with nothing left to lose. Within a year, most signed up for the Continental army.

Until 2000, the Jared Cone House was the only Bolton house to be on the National Register of Historic Places. Jared Cone built the largest house in Bolton in his day, but due to costs incurred in the American Revolution, he lost his house to creditors. It was a comfortable bed-and-breakfast for several years.

Another Bolton resident, Herman Baker, had also served in the Lexington Alarm. Later, on May 3, 1775, he joined the Fifth Company of the Second Continental Regiment and served as a sergeant. He was taken prisoner that winter at Quebec. By 1776, the movement toward independence was gathering momentum. On June 20, 1776, Jonathan Birge changed his commission from a captain under the Crown to a captain in the Continental army. General Washington then called for reinforcements and the Connecticut Assembly responded by ordering the enlistment of seven battalions, commanded by Brigadier General James Wadsworth. The Third Battalion of Wadsworth's Brigade was commanded by Colonel Comfort Sage and consisted of eight companies. The Fourth Company consisted of volunteers from the Bolton-Tolland area and was commanded by Captain Jonathan Birge. Herman Baker was paroled from the British prison at Quebec in August 1776, and immediately returned to Bolton to enlist and serve under Jonathan Birge as a corporal.

Captain Birge's company traveled the Revolutionary Route, and in September 1776, fought in the Battle of New York, resisting a full-scale invasion of British and Hessian forces under General Howe. Baker was again captured by the British on September 15, 1776. Washington made a strategic withdrawal and dug in the American lines at White Plains, New York. During the Battle of White Plains on October 28, 1776, Captain Birge was badly wounded and was allowed to try to return to Bolton. The Revolutionary Route was filled with refugees, the wounded leaving the embattled towns and fresh troops heading for the front. Captain Birge died and was buried in an unmarked grave near Stamford on November 10, 1776.

As a prisoner in New York in the notorious prison ships, Herman Baker came down with smallpox but survived to be released in January 1777. In his weakened condition, he traveled the Revolutionary Route, only to die on January 21, 1777, one day away from his home. His grave is next to Willow Brook on Willow Brook Road in East Hartford. The location is just inside the Pratt and Whitney property, just east of the first pumping station.

THE CONTINENTAL ARMY AND FRENCH ENCAMPMENTS

The discovery on Bolton Heritage Farm of regimental uniform buttons and cannon and musket balls from the Continental and French armies has helped raise the awareness of the importance of preserving the historic Washington-Rochambeau Route. As you come down Brandy Road to Bolton

Heritage Farm, you see the same historic vista today that Rochambeau and Washington saw in 1781. On the farm itself, you'll find an original colonial road lined with stone walls leading to a circular stone corral, which was for lost-and-found animals of the community. The officers of the French army thought the beauty of Bolton as well as its innocence was something to write home about.

Private Jeremiah Greenman kept a diary in which he traces the movements of the Continental army through Bolton on five different campaigns. On Friday, October 18, 1776, Private Greenman writes that Continental army troops breakfasted in Bolton on the way to the Quebec campaign. On April 12, 1777, he writes that Continental army troops camped in Bolton on a Saturday in rain and cold on the way to the Defense of the Delaware. On Thursday, January 29, 1778, Continental army troops from Valley Forge rested in Bolton on their way to study British positions in Rhode Island. On Monday, May 11, 1778, the Continental army troops stopped and fed their horses in Bolton on the way back to Valley Forge. On Tuesday, July 28, 1778, a troop movement of the Continental army (about one thousand men) stopped in Bolton and cooked up lunch on the way to the Battle of Rhode Island. Brigadier General James Mitchell Varnum led his brigade in addition to Colonel Henry Jackson's regiment. On the evening of Sunday, November 21, 1779, victorious Continental army troops returning from Rhode Island had dinner in Bolton and camped the night on the way to Valley Forge. With Boston and Rhode Island liberated, it was then safe for General Rochambeau to land our French allies at Newport, Rhode Island. On December 23, 1780, Continental army troops stopped in Bolton on the way to Rhode Island to meet the French.

"Expedition Particular" was the name of the French expedition of allied troops sent to assist the American colonies during the Revolutionary War. The symbol of the expedition was carried on the march. On Thursday, November 16, 1780, the Duc de Lauzun, commander of the French cavalry, wrote that he passed General Chastellux in Bolton as he rode with some of the French dragoons to Hartford.

On, November 16, 1780, Chastellux—a major general, Rochambeau's first officer, an enlightened man, a member of the French Academy and a perceptive observer of affairs in the new republic—wrote the following:

> *After descending a gentile slope for about two miles, I found myself in a rather narrow, but agreeable and well-cultivated valley: it is watered by a rivulet which flows into the "Sheunganick" and which is adorned with the name of "Hope" River; you follow this valley to Bolton.*

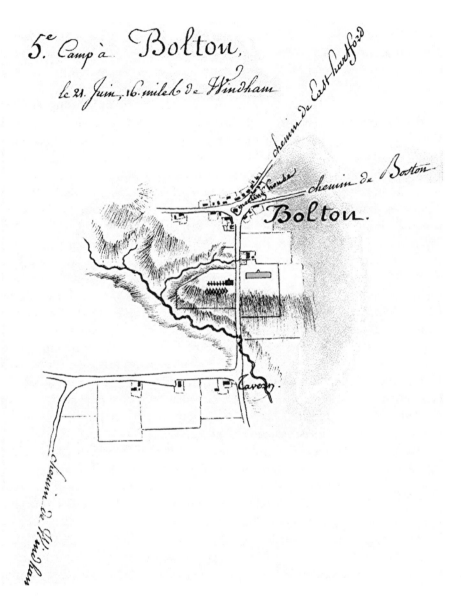

This map, rediscovered in 1994, made it clear that the previously believed location of the French army encampment in Bolton was incorrect. That led to state legislation to locate all of these campsites in Connecticut and, eventually, all of them on the Washington-Rochambeau Revolutionary Route. Now we have federal legislation proposed to make the whole route a National Historic Trail.

Until 1811, every labeled map showed that Bolton was the headwaters of the Hope River. A mapmaker in 1811 made a spelling error and the river thereafter became the Hop River.

In June 21–24, 1781, four French regiments of more than one thousand men each, under General Rochambeau, camped on the site of the present Bolton Heritage Farm. General Rochambeau was the guest of honor in the house of Reverend Colton.

Lieutenant Gabriel-Gaspard Baron de Gallatin of the Deux Ponts Regiment relates that in Bolton, "the band played outside the camp and we danced on the green."

Louis-Alexandre Berthier's wrote in his itinerary:

> *When within 4 miles of Bolton, you begin to encounter more houses. The road is then very close to the river. You cross a brook on a wooden bridge. There is a ford beside it and a sawmill on the left, then beyond the bridge turn left, then go through a small hamlet of scattered houses separated by several little brooks that flow down to the river. You leave on the left White's Tavern* [Hutchinson Road, Andover]. *You cross a few more brooklets. You go through a little wood where the road climbs sharply. This grade is very steep* [Bailey Road]. *At the top you turn sharp right* [on to Brandy Street] *and come to the first houses of Bolton. Bolton is a small town comprising many scattered houses, some of which are clustered around the meeting house on a spacious but low plateau. Through this part of Bolton runs a high road* [Bolton Center Road] *that goes left to Colchester and right to Boston. The Camp is to be located on this* [east] *side of the meeting house* [Bolton Heritage Farm].

Clermont-Crevecoeur, on June 21, 1781, noted after traveling through Bolton:

> *Bolton, a very small town, which is quite pretty. The roads were frightful, with mountains and very steep grades...We had entered the providence of Connecticut, one of the most productive in cattle, wheat, and every kind of commodity. It is unquestionably the most fertile province in America, for its soil yields everything necessary to life. The pasture is so good here that the cattle are of truly excellent quality. The beef is exceptionally good. The poultry and game are exquisite.*

GENERAL WASHINGTON'S ANSWER

The French army joined the American Continental army, marched down the Revolutionary Route and surrounded and shelled the British southern army at Yorktown. On October 19, 1781, the British southern army surrendered to General Washington and peace negotiations soon began in Paris. Several years later, President Washington and General Rochambeau both wrote that their armies had intentionally approached New York City first so that the British would reinforce New York City and not Yorktown. The Continental and French armies then quickly attacked and defeated the British at Yorktown.

General Rochambeau spent November 2, 1782, at the home of Reverend Colton and completed one of his report packets on the French military campaign in America. This letter is Washington's confirmation of receipt of the package.

Historic Tales

One question of the Revolutionary War was why after the victory at Yorktown did Washington, in 1782, order the French army to march north from Yorktown, and past New York City on the same route used to attack Yorktown? It is a question because the French army was about to be deployed in the Caribbean, so they could have sailed directly from Yorktown. The answer to the question is given in General Washington's response to a report that General Rochambeau sent from Bolton, Connecticut.

On November 4, 1782, Yale president Ezra Stiles visited with General Rochambeau at the home of Reverend George Colton in Bolton. Stiles records in his diary that he, Reverend Colton and General Rochambeau conversed that evening in Latin. At that time, Latin was still the common language spoken by all clergy, officers, diplomats, scientists and other educated people. That night Rochambeau finished a military report on the French involvement in the American Revolution and posted the packet from Bolton to General George Washington.

General Washington's answer to Rochambeau's Bolton letter shows that the reason for the French marching north on the Revolutionary Route was to again threaten the British army that still occupied New York City, so that the British would withdraw all their troops from the Southern cities (e.g. Charleston, South Carolina) to reinforce their army in New York City:

Head Quarters, November 12, 1782.

Sir:

I had the honor of receiving your Excellency's letter from Bolton in due time. The packet for the Minister of France which accompanied it was forwarded immediately.

We have no intelligence of the actual evacuation of Charlestown town, but from some circumstances which have appeared in the New York paper of the 5th. Instant, I think it probable that that event has taken place.

The moment I receive any information which may be depended on, I shall transmit it.

I have the honor etc.
G. Washington

And so it is clear that one objective of having the French army return on the Revolutionary Route through Bolton was so that Southern cities like Charleston would be liberated quickly without any further bloodshed.

A CHRISTMAS TRADITION

The Puritans who came to America were most inclined toward prayer, fasting and thanksgiving. But they must have also been a complex and conflicted people because they also helped run the rum-sugar-slave trade triangle for the British. Many religious sects frowned upon celebration, but the Pilgrims and other immigrants introduced Bolton to celebrations and feasts. Christmas to most early Bolton residents meant hunting and then feasting on meat pies. Our traditional Christmas, with Christmas trees and church choirs, gradually took hold during the 1800s. For as long as they burned, yule logs meant festive drinking, conviviality and freedom from farm work.

Eggnog is a descendant of a hot British drink of the elite, called posset, which consisted of eggs, milk and ale or wine, ingredients then too costly for the average man. But it was the colonists—with their access to dairy products, local liquor stills and affordable Caribbean rum—that changed the eggnog recipe forever and made it one of the most popular of American Christmas drinks. It was far more affordable than the heavily taxed brandy or other European spirits that it replaced at our ancestors' holiday revels. The first recorded mention of eggnog in colonial America points to its creation in Philadelphia sometime before 1796:

George Washington's Recipe for Eggnog:

One quart cream
One quart milk
One dozen tbsp. sugar or Sucanat (½ c.)
One pint brandy (2 c.)
½ pint rye whiskey (1 c.)
½ pint Jamaica rum (1 c.)
¼ pint sherry (½ c.)

Mix liquor first, then separate yolks and whites of eggs, add sugar to beaten yolks, and mix well. Add liquor to mixture drop by drop at first, slowly beating. Add milk and cream, slowly beating. Beat whites of eggs until stiff and fold slowly into mixture. Let set in cool place for several days. Taste frequently.

Sucanat was dehydrated sugar cane with little to no processing—an excellent source of iron, calcium, vitamin B6, potassium and chromium. Like many of our ancestors who handed down the family recipes, Washington neglected to mention one important detail. While he was clear on the exact amount of brandy, whiskey, rum and sherry to be used, he failed to include the number of eggs. So for that part, it has been suggested to use eight eggs, separated.

Oh, and don't forget to save the trunk of the Christmas tree for next year's yule logs!

ELECTION DAY TRADITIONS

Connecticut has a unique history of government. In 1636, Thomas Hooker led the first Connecticut settlers from Massachusetts through Bolton to finally settle in Hartford. Finding themselves without a charter, they established a set of laws, the Fundamental Orders. At their first election, in 1638, Reverend Hooker preached a sermon about the privilege of election, which he said belongs to the people but must be exercised according to the will and law

One Bolton election day tradition was to celebrate all day. The presidential election of 1916 was particularly exciting, as incumbent Woodrow Wilson promised to keep America out of World War I, and narrowly won against Supreme Court Justice Charles Hughes. The war had been raging in Europe for the past two years. It was the first presidential vote taken in the new town hall, and by then only a few people still traveled by one-horsepower vehicles.

of God. To those unfamiliar with Puritan beliefs, the sermon appeared to be a new liberal assertion against autocratic rule. It was, in fact, the Puritan doctrine.

While the Puritan religion was normally of a very serious nature, Election Day was a day of celebration and of baking cakes. The tradition stuck. By the mid-1800s, after a trip to the polls, large groups met throughout Connecticut to celebrate the election returns. Election Day guests were served yeast cakes accompanied by eggnog or punch. The traditional evening menu might also include homemade sausages, hot biscuits, fried green apples and blueberry preserves. While skepticism of election promises has grown, there are still times when the issues are great and the turnout is enthusiastically large, such as the four-way race in 1916, two years after the new Bolton Town Hall was built. Town hall was decked out in red, white and blue that year.

Our unique, traditional Election Day recipe survives to this day in many New England cookbooks. The following recipe is from *The Yankee Cook Book,* by Imogene Wolcott, who explains that Election Cake is said to have originated in Hartford, Connecticut, and was "served to all who voted the straight ticket."

Election Day Cake

> *2 cups milk, scalded*
> *¾ cup shortening*
> *½ cup brown sugar, tightly packed*
> *2 eggs*
> *½ teaspoon salt*
> *1½ cups raisins*
> *1 compressed yeast cake*
> *¼ pound citron sliced thin (optional)*
> *½ teaspoon nutmeg*
> *5 cups flour sifted*
> *½ teaspoon mace*
> *1½ cups sugar*

Place milk, brown sugar and salt in a mixing bowl. When lukewarm add crumbled yeast cake and 4½ cups of the flour; beat thoroughly and let rise overnight. In the morning cream the sugar and shortening and add. Stir in the eggs, raisins, citron, nutmeg, mace and remaining ½ cup flour. Mix thoroughly using hands if necessary. Place in greased bread tins lined with waxed paper and again greased. Rise until double in bulk. Bake in a moderately hot oven (375° F) until brown, about 50 minutes. Makes 2 loaves.

It was customary for many years to take Election Day off and celebrate the right to vote all day. Oh, and don't forget to vote!

Part IV

The Cathedrals of Bolton

When we think of cathedrals, we think of places that open new feelings in the human soul, filling it with eagerness, joy, hope, inspiration and yearning. Many people, not necessarily religious, find a source of deep spiritual refreshment in visits to great cathedrals. There is something about cathedrals that draws in even the most detached among us. Cathedrals put us in touch with something larger and grander than ourselves and much more powerful than our fears. They are among those things that endure, and in a world of seemingly interminable change we gravitate to such places. Indeed, we hunger for them, because eternity seems palpable in such places.

THE CATHEDRALS OF BOLTON

Bolton's natural beauty is primarily the work of the last glacier that moved through and gouged out amphitheaters, sanctuaries, altars and sacristies. Then as it retreated, it left many stone pillars, beautiful façades and rock sculptures. We have read the words of many people who attest in their diaries, published letters and books that they experienced our cathedrals of natural heritage while they themselves were making history.

Anyone who has ever strolled through the fields of the Bolton Heritage Farm, who sees the stone walls at their feet, and a living carpet reaching into the distance with the big sky overhead, knows that these fields and forests are as much a part of our heritage as any of the world's other great cathedrals. The Great Awakening begun by Jonathan Edwards occurred after his

Gay City was set up by a religious commune (Society of Gilead). It was said that Gay City folk caught a horse thief, tied him to this tree and gave him twenty stripes with the lash. French Road was originally a back way into Gay City.

An unidentified Bolton farm family poses in Sunday clothes with their favorite domesticated animals. These were among the last families to farm with very little machinery, before there was electricity and gasoline engines.

epiphany while walking in these fields of Bolton in 1723. Almost everyone from seniors to new homeowners worked in 2000 to preserve this farm near the town center of Bolton.

Another later period of revival renewed interest in the Creator and spawned a new form of religious expression—the camp meeting. The very first New England camp meeting was held right here in another great cathedral of Bolton. This amphitheater is a precious natural wonder, part of a stunning wetlands complex covering much of the southeast section of Bolton. It was created for us to stand and look at in awe. It is hard, rough and wet, but totally suitable for rendering the pure delight that awakens, opens and ennobles human nature. It contains the essence of that which is needed to sustain the land with fresh water, and to filter and scent our air. Bolton was chosen for the first camp meeting in New England in 1805 because Bolton had this great cathedral that could hold the nine thousand worshipers who visited that week. The Bolton Land Trust saved this great cathedral in 2004.

Many residents still climb Bolton Notch (Saqumsketuck) in the fall to be dazzled by the colors, just as the Mohegan were. There, on the sacred craggy outcrop of rock, was the forward lookout used by the mighty Uncas. That cathedral was saved as Bolton Notch Park and Freja Park.

Gay City Hollow is another cathedral sited partially in Bolton that was settled by the Society of Giliad in the early 1800s. It has also been saved as a state park. The back road out was French Road in Bolton, where there were several fertile farms and a whipping tree, too—for tying up horse thieves.

We are drawn to these cathedrals, where living water wells up, cold and pure, from the earth's dark bosom. And we sense there is something deeper and more complex in Bolton's cathedrals. There are sacred grounds within them. For many, it is a pleasure to stand in awe of these great cathedrals of earth, with their pillars of rock, carpets of ferns, choirs of streams, altars of stone and vaults of skies and stars. We sense as the Mohegan still do, Mundo wigo…God is great.

There is a wind blowing in Bolton to preserve Bolton's smaller cathedrals as well. It actually costs less to save them than to allow them to be destroyed by development. After we have been here a while, we discover that we don't just chose to live in Bolton, it chooses us and then it rouses our dormant spirits to take action to save our heritage. We were guided once by Mohegan

Children sit in their new one-horse shay with a young pony, circa 1880.

footpaths to settle in Bolton but now we seem to be guided ever more by the spiritual paths of the Mohegan.

THE FIRST NEW ENGLAND CAMP MEETING

A period of religious revival began in 1795 that spawned a new form of religious expression—the camp meeting. This revival was the precursor to the Second Great Awakening, which focused more on the heart and inspired a wave of social reform that gave rise to abolitionist groups and temperance campaigns, as well as efforts to reform prisons and care for the handicapped and mentally ill.

Camp meetings became the Woodstocks of the Second Awakening and were the reason that revivalism reached the sparsely settled areas of early America. These events were held in the open air and took place over several days because attendees had to travel many miles, camping in tents, covered wagons, and makeshift shelters of brush. They would cook over open fires and attend the services throughout the morning, afternoon and evening.

People were asked to let go of their burdens and rededicate themselves to God. It is believed that the first camp meeting was held at Red River, Kentucky, in June 1800. A much larger one was held at Cane Ridge, Kentucky, in August 1801, where between ten thousand and twenty-five thousand people attended.

The first camp meeting in New England was held in Bolton for three days beginning June 30, 1805, in the southeastern area of our town, near the Andover town line. The roads to the area were later abandoned and the site was all but forgotten. The famous Lorenzo Dow was the main speaker, and it was estimated that between six thousand and nine thousand people camped in Bolton at a time when the total population of Bolton was under two thousand people.

There appeared to have been no lack of preachers and praying laborers, no lack of variety in the flood of fervent oratory each day and no lack of exhortations, readings and testimonies of experiences. Families and individuals throughout the area would travel to camp together and meet for fellowship. Later there were camp meetings in the west of Bolton in 1836, 1838 and 1847, which resulted in the road there being named Camp Meeting Road.

Lorenzo Dow was born on October 16, 1777, in Coventry, Connecticut, where he was educated in a one-room schoolhouse. He died in Washington, D.C., in 1834. His wife Peggy, to whom he was married in 1804, was his constant traveling companion. She died in Hebron, Connecticut, on January 6, 1820.

Reverend Dow began his ministry at age eighteen. When he came to Bolton in 1805, he was twenty-eight and at the height of his fame. His early religious convictions led him to embrace the doctrines of the Methodists. In 1798, the Connecticut Conference received him. In 1799, they sent him to Cambridge, New York, and after a few months to Pittsfield, Massachusetts, and from there to Essex, Vermont, all within one year. He desired no permanent assignment but preferred to travel, as Christ's disciples had been instructed to spread the Gospel.

Dow became a well-known preacher who, in his lifetime, traveled to all seventeen of the states of the union as well as to Canada, England, Wales and Ireland. He probably spoke the Gospel to more persons than any other individual until Billy Graham. He was one of the most remarkable men of his age, known for his zeal and energy directed for the cause of God. His eccentric dress, style of preaching and fearless behavior attracted great attention, while his understanding of human character gave him

This photo of Methodist pastor Reverend J.M. Von Deck and his family was taken June 16, 1906. Quarryville was later known as Belknap.

considerable influence over the multitudes who attended his services. While he never had a permanent church or followers, there were few who doubted his true religion or good intentions.

He was restless and he was a dreamer. He was contradictory and never happier than when engaged in a war of words. His features were both rough and delicate, but in that face there was every mark of indomitable energy. He parted his hair in the middle and wore it hanging down to his shoulders. His face was radiant with kindness. His wife Peggy described her first meeting with him: "He is a most singular character, and admits himself that he was known by the name of 'Crazy Dow' and called himself 'Son of Thunder.'"

She also described their life on the road: "At night we camped out in lonely deserts, uninhabited by any being except wild beasts and savages...I was much alarmed and uneasy, but my husband was content and slept sweetly."

THE QUARRYVILLE BOOMTOWN

Bolton Notch, through which the highways and the railroad have forced their way, was probably a preglacial stream channel, later used as the outlet for a glacial stream to the east, at a time when the Connecticut valley was blocked by ice or glacial debris. It appears the notch followed a fault fracture that made the rock easier to erode and later easier to quarry. The rock is known as Bolton schist, whose layers can best be seen along the railway cut. Immediately west of the gorge, you drop down across a fault plane to the Connecticut valley sandstone.

Much of this scenic spot is now preserved in parks consisting of 116 acres. The region has many Native American associations. Located in the park is Squaw Cave, an old Mohegan spring, and Black Sal's Cave, once the home of a Mohegan family.

Quarryville was centered around Bolton Notch Hollow. The area was once a bustling boomtown echoing with the hoarse shouts of men splitting veins of granite and flagstone. Rum and religion clashed to influence the tough, big-handed men who worked and played hard in the hollow.

The first mention of a route through the notch was by French General Chastellux on November 4, 1782. He took it as a shortcut to Coventry to avoid Bolton Center, which was filled with French troops that day. He said it cut three miles of the Post Road route. The Bolton Historical Society has a quarry contract that was written by Elijah Phillips with quill pen on parchment in 1809. Phillips was one of the well-known bully boys who employed and worked with quarrymen before the railroad came.

By 1840, when this picture was taken, 85 percent of the Connecticut forests had been cut down and Squaw's Cave was completely exposed to view. Caves and old wells proved to be dangerous, so many were blasted, blocked or covered over. Today more than 70 percent of the forest has grown back and the cave is difficult to find.

In 1830, Quarryville was thriving and Bolton Notch had not yet been cut too deep. Here a quarry stone is being taken to Hartford, and the worker's wife and family watch as he goes by.

Bolton granite was of high quality and in demand. The flagstone was a fine micaceous slate use for walkways, doorstops and school blackboards. Fine Bolton quarry stone was used in Hartford, for the Springfield Armory and as far away as New York, Albany, Philadelphia, Baltimore and Washington. Millstones in 1812 weighed between four and five thousand pounds and sold for two cents a pound. The heavy slate and flagstone were taken by ox cart to the Connecticut River for shipment.

By 1820, Quarryville had assumed the status of a village and was becoming as important as Bolton Center. Taverns flourished under Colonel Chester Daggett, Elijah Fitch and Jonas Maine. Unlike the earlier Bolton Post Road taverns, which were primarily inns where strangers often shared beds or slept on the floor, these new taverns were places to drink and, seemingly, to make pacts with the devil. These were the kinds of taverns that sparked the temperance movement.

Before the railroad came to Bolton, the notch cut was only about forty feet deep. From 1847 to 1849, Turner Stevens led a team of hardy men who blasted the first deep east and west railroad cuts through the notch.

When Bolton was settled, the notch was shallow and the climb to the pass was steep. That is why the road went though Bolton Center until after the railroad. There were two other major deep cuts made over the years, one to lower the railroad bed and the other for a major widening to fit the highway.

Everyone working for the railroad was flush with thirty dollars in pay each month. The old Notch Hollow dance hall stood opposite the train depot and resounded with the fiddling of "Waltz Me Around Again Willie" and other popular tunes of the time. A clubhouse for traveling railroad executives was built just west of Quarryville. The Quarryville Post Office opened in 1848, and moved quickly to the railroad depot. Later the Rainbow Club opened near where Georgina's Restaurant now stands. In the Bolton Notch Pond photo, it is shown in the distance beyond Bolton Pond.

By 1913, the Norwich Turnpike was redirected from Bolton Center to the notch, where twenty-six buildings, including homes, a soap factory (Martin Chemical Co.), a grocery store, grain sheds and coal-weighing scales, filled the hollow with activity. Quarryville had grown along the lake and extended to the area of the Methodist Church built in 1852. The last railroad improvement in Bolton was the second notch railroad cut in 1929.

Bolton Notch Pond borders Freja Park. This scene is looking from the notch and over the pond some time between 1890 and 1920. At the bottom are the train station and grocery store shown in other photos. The ice storage house is seen on the opposite side of the pond. Farther away can be seen the Rainbow Club, where Georgina's Restaurant stands today.

Eshaw's Groceries existed in the notch in the early 1900s, and can also be seen in the picture of Bolton Pond with the icehouse and the Rainbow Club.

In 1832, Bolton resident Patten Fitch came up with the idea of providing controlled water power to the mills in Willimantic by damming up Cedar Swamp, thereby creating Bolton Lake. This deprived Bolton of its primary source of water power because the water flowed at night in Bolton to supply power to the mills in Willimantic during daylight. That worked for many years until the dam's sluice gate fell victim to rust and it became impossible to regulate water flow. The Bolton Lake dam held until the hurricane of 1938, which took Bolton by surprise. Since the sluice gate could not be opened further to handle the floodwaters, the water flowed over the dam and washed it out. The raging wall of mud, stone and water took out five hundred feet of roads, closing Stony Road, South Road and South Street in Coventry, depositing the debris in Andover. Luckily, there were no houses in the path. Federal funds were used to rebuild the dam in 1941, but it leaked and immediately washed out a second time and had to be rebuilt. Today, with only one of the original Quarryville buildings remaining, Notch Hollow is a ghost of its booming past.

The Second Awakening and a Bolton Tragedy

Caregivers, doctors, nurses and pastors are those most exposed to illness today, just as they were in the past. In the early 1800s, the cause of typhus was unknown, and after someone died, his clothes and bedding were often burned. In one small European country, 40 percent of the doctors died while trying to contain an outbreak of typhus.

In the early 1800s, Asahel Nettleton began the Second Great Awakening here in Connecticut. His classmate at Yale, Philander Parmelee, was his best friend through life and became the fifth Congregational Church pastor of Bolton. While in college, Yale president Timothy Dwight, the grandson of Jonathan Edwards, took note of Nettleton and remarked, "He will make one of the most useful men this country has ever seen."

While the intellectual Jonathan Edwards had started the First Great Awakening, Asahel Nettleton began the type of revival that we see today. He was often invited to speak to congregations, where his probing questions left people wondering how he knew their very deepest secrets and left them worrying that they had condemned themselves. Town-wide revivals usually followed him. He was so carefully studied and well imitated by some of his peers that he has been largely forgotten while his best imitators are remembered.

In a personal letter to Philander Parmelee dated August 4, 1815, Nettleton recounted what happened when he spoke at a local school for girls in New Haven:

For three days the distress of some was overwhelming. On the fourth day four were rejoicing. On the fifth day eleven more were rejoicing. From that time the work has been gradually spreading through the town…Within about four weeks upwards of fifty have entertained hope in this place.

Similarly, he wrote to Pastor Parmelee from Middletown on December 1, 1817:

They [the people at his meeting] *left the house and went home sighing & sobbing in every direction. I came home & found a number around the door of Mr. Williams' house, in the most awful distress, some were standing, some sitting on the ground, & some on the door steps exclaiming "What shall I do? I shall die. I shall die. I can't live!" Within a few days 8 or 10 are rejoicing in hope. What will be the end, I know not. Do pray for us, and your friend, A. Nettleton.*

The Brick Tavern served the public from about 1815 to 1850. Bolton artist Susan Bosworth painted the house with the flower gardens as seen in the recent past. The Brick Tavern is on the National Register of Historic Places.

The Brick Tavern is shown circa 1815–22, with the church and a small house that was later replaced by the Hutchinson house, where former Town Clerk Olive Toomey grew up. The house on the right served at times as a grocery store and a post office. The previous town historian, Larry Larned, lived there for several years.

In early October 1822, Nettleton visited a family in Wilbraham, Massachusetts, where he contracted typhus fever. His friend Philander and wife Abigail took him in and nursed him in Bolton, Connecticut, in the original parish house in which General Washington had dined and Rochambeau had slept just forty-one years earlier. By December, Nettleton began to recover, only to discover that his kind and loving hosts, the Parmelees, had contracted the disease themselves. Abigail recovered but Reverend Philander succumbed to the disease on December 27. That broke Nettleton's heart, and he described that time as the most trying of his life. It was two years before he could resume his work. He was never the same and his imitators had supplanted him by then.

The records indicate that Abigail remained in the original Bolton colonial house for a while and then it was abandoned for a few years. The typhus incident was lost from Bolton memory until recently.

THE BRICK TAVERN

At one time, a small cigar factory stood where the town hall now stands between the church and the Brick Tavern on the town green. The Hartford–Norwich stage line ran on the Norwich Turnpike down Bolton Center Road and Watrous Road. The stagecoach stopped at the Brick Tavern, which still stands today at 220 Bolton Center Road. Reverend Colton performed his last wedding, that of Sarah White to Samuel Williams, on March 12, 1812. Samuel Williams came to Bolton in 1809 and built the Brick Tavern. He also built the new parsonage on Hebron Road after the untimely death of Reverend Parmelee.

The Brick Tavern was built near to the church because stagecoach taverns were still respectable at that time. It was the town motel. Dr. Charles F. Sumner settled in Bolton in 1842, and said that, until 1851, Bolton sometimes sustained as many as four taverns. Inn owners like Dr. Sumner were still among the town's most prominent citizens although the reputation of taverns was declining.

The construction of the railroad in 1850 soon ended the age of the stagecoach, the Bolton taverns and much of the importance of Bolton roads for interstate commerce. That is one of the reasons why many of Bolton's historic sites and natural heritage have survived until today. The Town of Bolton purchased the Brick Tavern with twenty-two acres at the heart of Bolton in 2007.

It was discovered early on that Bolton shade tobacco made excellent cigar wrappers. The skyline of Bolton changed when the Sumners built a cigar factory where the town hall now stands, between the Brick Tavern and the Congregational Church, circa 1852.

Part V

Civil War Bolton

In 1830, Britain abolished its international slave trade and pressure was mounting to end slavery throughout the world. In 1838, Abraham Lincoln's Lyceum speech indicated that he thought that the slavery issue could destroy the United States from within. Washington and the other Founding Fathers had captured the hearts and minds of the American people, but the slavery compromise that was needed to make the Declaration of Independence acceptable to all thirteen colonies had left a spot on America's ideals. America had created in its government a system of political institutions conducive to what was necessary to ensure civil and religious liberty. This is the birthright of every American, a great gift given to us that we did not earn. We are the legal inheritors of liberty and civil rights from our founding fathers, who had turned the world upside down to give them to us.

Lincoln saw that the issue of slavery was a spot of tyranny left from earlier governments that made a sham of equal rights and civil liberty. The profaning of America's basic ideals impoverished and threatened to destroy America's soul from within.

Furthermore, President Lincoln saw that the purpose of each generation of Americans is to transmit these ideals unspoiled to the next generation. He said Americans do that out of gratitude to our Founding Fathers, for justice to ourselves and as a duty to posterity. He said it is out of our love for mankind that Americans cannot abandon America's ideals. That was the tone he set for centuries to come.

CHARLES LYMAN, BOLTON CIVIL WAR HERO

Born April 10, 1843, to Jacob and Dorcas Lyman of Bolton, Charles Lyman attended a one-room schoolhouse in Bolton during the winter and worked as a farmhand during the summer. By sixteen, he was a teacher at the Birch Mountain Schoolhouse. At age nineteen, he finished his formal education, taking one term at Rockville High School and then volunteering to fight in President Lincoln's army on July 21, 1862.

Forty-eight young men of Bolton, roughly 7 percent of Bolton's population, marched off as parts of four regiments. The Sixteenth was the "hard luck" regiment—the others had no luck at all. There were no "lucky" regiments, just survivors. Charles was in the Fourteenth and they were called to duty on August 20, 1861, just four days before the "hard luck" regiment. They had almost no training when they arrived for the Battle of Antietam (Sharpsburg), Maryland, the bloodiest single-day battle in American history. Fortunately, the Bolton soldiers—with their education, hard farm work, self-reliance, survival skills and hunting skills—were somewhat prepared to survive the war.

Charley, a corporal, was almost killed on his first day of battle on September 17, 1862. Mary Bedinger Mitchell described what the battle sounded like down the road:

It is curious how much louder guns sound when they are pointed at you than when they are turned the other way! And the shell, with its long-drawn screeching, doubtless more terrifying than the singing minie-ball, has a way of making one's hair stand on end.

The Union army attacked through the woods, moving into a forty-acre cornfield. The heavy volleys of fire from the Rebel lines had a particular sound that Lieutenant Frederick Hitchcock described as he approached the battlefield: "These volleys of musketry we were approaching sounded in the distance like the rapid pouring of shot upon a tin pan, or the tearing of heavy canvas, with slight pauses interspersed with single shots, or desultory shooting."

The shots took a heavy toll from the regiment, and in the midst of the battle the sound was described as the whistling song of Confederate minié balls. They almost reached the high ground when the sound changed again. Artillery and exploding canister were unleashed, devouring the green soldiers. Alpheus Williams described that noise:

The roar of the infantry was beyond anything conceivable...If all the stone and brick houses of Broadway [New York City] *should tumble at once the roar and rattle could hardly be greater, and amidst this, hundreds of pieces of artillery, right and left, were thundering as a sort of bass section of the infernal music.*

The Fourteenth Regiment was advancing in a suicide charge when a Confederate shell burst less than three feet from Charley, killing four and wounding five others and stunning, but only scratching, Charley. The lucky dust of Bolton was still on him. After picking up the body parts and burying the dead, Charley was shipped off to fight at Fredericksburg, Virginia. But the commanders had noticed how skilled and calm Charley was, and unbeknownst to him, they were already starting paperwork to make him a second lieutenant.

On December 13, 1862, the Fourteenth Regiment was at Fredericksburg in another suicide charge on a Rebel position at Marye's Heights. Charley was so focused that he did not notice his regiment was already retreating under the withering fire. The four in this unit closest to him had fallen farther back and he was within about two hundred yards of the Rebel camp command post, not knowing he was alone. Then he saw a Confederate officer come out of his command post, which was in the Stevens House. Charley fired twice and missed the officer but attracted attention as if he had thrown a hornet's nest into the Rebel camp.

Bullets were buzzing around him as he finally stopped advancing and stood behind a four-inch-wide fence post just in time for the post to stop a bullet from hitting him in the stomach. Charley was too focused on shooting that Rebel officer to notice that he was now the only Union soldier fighting the entire Rebel army. He rested his rifle on the post to steady his aim, but before he could squeeze the trigger a bullet struck the stock of his rifle and flew over his right shoulder. Again he took aim and fired a third round, this time hitting the officer. Now the Rebels were really angry because the officer was General Cobb, who rapidly bled to death. Charley at last looked around and saw he was the only one the Rebels were shooting at because the others were almost back to safety. He wrote, "Bullets were flying very thick about me and I had no expectation of getting off the field alive, as it was fully 300 yards to the nearest cover."

Charley ran toward a canal, where there was a foundation that had been dug for an icehouse. A bullet went through his haversack and the skirt of his overcoat, and a shell burst right over his head. Just before he reached cover, he felt as though a horse had kicked him in the back. Charley dropped into the hole. He had been shot in the back.

Fortunately, Charley had been carrying all his heavy equipment on his back and the musket shot spent its energy tearing through fourteen layers of his wool blanket and never touched him. But Jerry Gready, from neighboring Vernon, Connecticut, was in that hole, too, and as he fled the field a bullet entered his heel and came out between his toes. Charley attended to him and about one hundred wounded men for the rest of the day, and when darkness fell, he carried Jerry on his back to the Union field hospital.

By February 1863, Charles Lyman was promoted to second lieutenant and again, unbeknownst to him, his papers for his promotion to first lieutenant were already in the works. More remarkably, however, twenty-year-old Second Lieutenant Charles Lyman was immediately put in command of a different company, passing over first lieutenants and experienced soldiers, some of whom were jealous, had high connections and began plotting against Charley. This was the worst thing and the best thing that happened to him at that time.

When in the next battle a young man named Starkey died, his father, who had fought side by side with his son, asked Lieutenant Charles Lyman for a leave of absence to bury his son and asked him to write a short obituary. Charley showed the other officers what he had written and they all agreed that it was a common practice and that it did not violate any new orders. But when he gave it to Starkey's father, Charley found himself court-martialed. One of the jealous officers took the letter from Starkey's father and sent it to the War Department, claiming Charles Lyman had violated the most recent secrecy orders.

The War Department acted without a hearing, and did not tell Charley the specific charge. It was a time when the War Department was rounding up Union deserters and putting them in front of firing squads, and the first draft of soldiers was being considered. Charley didn't think it was wise to make trouble by asking what the charge was, so he ended up with a dishonorable discharge on May 12, 1863, after only nine months of active duty. At the age of twenty, he was back teaching young ladies. Truly, Charley's bad luck was better than what half the young soldiers were longing for at that moment in history.

Charley married Amelia Campbell of Hartford in 1865, and they had two children. He attended a business college and landed a job in the Treasury Department in Washington, D.C. Once in Washington, he resolved to clear his name with the help of officers who knew of his heroism. He wrote directly to President Ulysses Grant, and within a few days his dismissal was revoked and he received his honorable discharge. In 1872, President Grant appointed him as civil service examiner for the treasury.

Civil War–era lucky Charles Lyman.

In 1875, he graduated as class valedictorian from National University Law School. President Chester Arthur promoted him to chief examiner.

President Grover Cleveland then promoted him to the Civil Service Commission. President Benjamin Harrison reappointed him to the Civil Service Commission, along with a young Theodore Roosevelt. Together with Teddy Roosevelt, Charley cleaned out government corruption and cronyism. When corrupt politicians tried to smear his name by saying he had been dishonorably discharged, the *New York Times* came to his defense on May 13, 1883. He was the commission chairman from 1886 to 1893. This commission established the first merit system for federal workers whose jobs previously had gone to political hacks appointed for their support in political campaigns. Later, he served as the chief of appointments for the secretary of the treasury.

Charles Lyman became a friend of Teddy Roosevelt, belonged to the Sons of the American Revolution, the Evangelical Alliance and the Washington City Bible Society, and was an active member of the Republican Party. Booker T. Washington's papers show that after the Civil War, Charles Lyman helped him find jobs for educated former slaves. Charles Lyman is a son of Bolton of whom we can all be proud.

A BLOODY BOLTON STORY

The Civil War was the bloodiest war on earth until World War I, and it was America's second war that pitted brother against brother. More soldiers died in Civil War battles and prisons than most European nations had enlisted in their armies. Consider that the twenty-five thousand troops Great Britain had stationed in America to suppress the Revolution was Britain's largest expeditionary force deployed overseas up until World War I. Hearing of the American Civil War casualties convinced many nations that they did not ever want to become America's enemy.

The Sixteenth Connecticut Regiment was formed in July and August 1862. It was mustered into service August 24, 1862, and became part of Lincoln's Army of the Potomac. Nearly 475 men in their prime were mustered into the service and from this group, 131 emaciated worn and shaken men returned to muster out of service in April 1865. Austin Tullar was thirty-two years old with a wife, three children and a two-month-old baby in Bolton when he left with the all-volunteer "hard luck" regiment. The regiment flag, and the camaraderie of the soldiers of this regiment, would forever change the meaning of the lives of Austin and his fellow soldiers.

Many of the recruits were from the privileged families of Hartford. Locals joked that they had to go to war without their servants. The officers and noncommissioned were either elected or politically appointed. Their only regular army officer was Colonel Frank Beach. They would serve in the first two battles under incompetent generals, whom President Lincoln would have to relieve from duty.

Bolton offered up a dozen of its finest to serve. This was what appeared to be a great adventure opening up for these young men. They wore their new, heavy, blue wool uniforms with shining brass buttons. They would probably be home for Christmas with some great war stories to tell.

They boarded the *City of Hartford* and the *Geo C. Collins* and sailed down the Connecticut River to New York, where they transferred to the steamer *Kill Van Kull* for the trip to New Jersey. From there they traveled overland to Baltimore. They received no discipline, not a single drill, and few instructions. On September 7, they had their first inspection under arms. This is when they were each issued a muzzleloader Springfield Model 1861 rifled musket. The Springfield fired a new bone-shattering projectile that resulted in the large number of amputations necessary during the war. This green regiment—with inexperienced officers, newly issued arms, heavy wool uniforms and no training—was put into its first battle just three weeks after leaving their loved ones. The regiment joined Harland's Second Brigade, Third Division of General Burnside's Ninth Army Corps. They loaded muskets for the first time only the day before their first battle. It was the Battle of Antietam, the bloodiest single-day battle in American history, with almost twenty-three thousand casualties.

At 10:00 a.m., General Burnside received orders from General McClellan to cross Antietam Creek and attack the Rebels. There was a delay in getting the movement orders to the Second Brigade, the only experienced regiment. That left the Sixteenth Connecticut and Fourth Rhode Island, two green regiments, in the vanguard of the battle. The Sixteenth moved up to the line with Captain Frederick H Barber (from Manchester) and Company H. This left the Sixteenth on the extreme left of the line, vulnerable to being outflanked. The battle line was formed to be able to concentrate the fire of the rifles into the mass of enemy before it. If the enemy came from another direction, an experienced line would wheel, facing the new threat. But the Sixteenth had no experience.

The Sixteenth waded across a creek in waist-deep water and took positions on the slope of a hill on the farm of J.H. Snively. Suddenly the Sixteenth fell under the sharpshooter fire of the Rebel batteries. The cannonade became furious as General Longstreet's entire rebel artillery started firing. Solid shot swept the crest of the hill in front and tore up the ground behind. Shells burst overhead, showering the Sixteenth with fragments of grape and canister. They fired packaged small-round shot that burst after leaving the cannon muzzle, forming a cloud of deadly missiles. Then suddenly the situation turned desperate, as they were ordered to stand at attention in front of what effectively was a Rebel firing squad.

B.F. Blakelee recounts:

> *While we were lying here, we were suddenly ordered to stand at attention, when a terrible volley was fired into us from behind a stone wall, about twenty five yards in front of us. We were ordered to fix bayonets and advance. In a moment we were riddled with shot. Many orders were given, which were not understood. Neither the line officers nor the men had any knowledge of regimental movements. The most helpless confusion ensued.*

Another regiment rushed panic-stricken past them to the rear. The Rebels quickly discovered the disorder and attacked in a heavy column. The Sixteenth and the Fourth Rhode Island were swept by a destructive fire. The order was given to fall back and this was done with some panic on the part of these green troops. Though 940 men had crossed Antietam Creek that morning, only 210 were present when regrouping near the creek later in the day. After sunset, the brigade moved back across the river to retire for the night. Sleep was difficult due to the cries and groans of the wounded and dying on the battlefield.

Every church, barn and house in the region became a field hospital. In the typical field hospital room, about twelve feet wide and twenty feet long, a bloody table stood near a window and around it stood the surgeons. A wounded man was laid on the table and it took but a few minutes to do what had to be done. The amputated limbs were thrown out of a window. John Snavely wrote that the "arms and legs were piled several feet high outside the Dunkerd Church window where the amputating tables sat."

From a single hospital in just that one day, there were as many as two cartloads of amputated legs, feet, arms and hands. Disabled men, such as Bolton's wounded Austin Tullar, were put to work carrying the most critically wounded, making beds of straw, hauling and cutting wood and assisting in a world reduced to bedlam. From the walls echoed the moans of the wounded, the gasping of the dying and the hymns for those for whom the dying was done. The yards and fields outside were strewn with straw, and the recovering patients were laid there without shelter through the September night.

On September 18, 1862, Austin Tullar and others in the Sixteenth were assigned to collect the body parts from the fields and trees, and bury them in mass graves. Many of the wounded were sent home as unfit for duty, and in the paperwork confusion, some were reported missing or as deserters and received no salary or medical help. On September 19, Austin Tullar was reported missing.

The casualties of the Sixteenth were later so high in December at Fredericksburg that the unit was pulled from the front lines and sent as reserves to Fort Williams at Plymouth, North Carolina. The fort had an escape route that was well protected by Federal gunboats. But then, in an unexpected massive ground and naval assault, the Rebels attacked the fort, captured the Federal gunboats and turned their guns on the fort. Though bombarded from every direction, General Wessels thought it would be a disgrace to surrender. As all hope of survival died, the men of the Sixteenth Connecticut tore their battle flag into shreds and distributed the remnants among the regiment, so it would not fall into the hands of the Rebels. They concealed these remnants on their bodies. The battle flag to them had become the symbol of what they meant to each other and of the Union of states for which they fought.

The Wilfred Maxwell House, located on School Road where it meets Brandy Street, looked quite different in 1890. The family posed in Sunday clothes with their surrey and fine horse.

The fort fell and the survivors were sent to the notorious Andersonville Confederate death camp, where more died than at Antietam. When finally freed, the Sixteenth Connecticut was recognized by General Ulysses S. Grant, and appointed his personal escort on the occasion of his visit to Raleigh, North Carolina, in April 1865.

In 1879, the remaining remnants of the battle flag of the Sixteenth were gathered together from the survivors and sewn onto a white silk banner. The resurrected remnants formed the blue shield surrounded by the American eagle. They trimmed it with a gold fringe and had the names of the battles fought by the Sixteenth emblazoned across the banner in gold. On Battle Flag Day, September 17, 1879, all the battle flags went on display at the Connecticut state capitol and can be seen to this day.

Austin Tullar was a disabled Bolton war veteran of the Sixteenth and proudly and patriotically named his eighth child Grant Colfax Tullar, after the new American president Ulysses S. Grant and vice president Schuyler Colfax. His son went on to become the famous music publisher Grant Colfax Tullar. Austin's wife Rhoda died in 1871, at age thirty-three, after their ninth and tenth children, twins, were born. Austin and his ten children were then desperately poor, and eventually he had to give up support of his children to his wife's family. No one knew that when Austin returned home an invalid from Antietam, the government declared him missing and later declared him a deserter. He may have lived without medical help out of fear of execution if he ever tried to clear his name as lucky Charles Lyman had. Perhaps one day his name can be cleared, too, knowing what he and "hard luck" regiment volunteers sacrificed for a United States of America.

GRANT TULLAR, MUSIC PUBLISHER

Grant Colfax Tullar was born August 5, 1869, in Bolton, Connecticut. He was named after President Ulysses S. Grant and Vice President Schuyler Colfax. His father was a proud, patriotic veteran of the American Civil War and unable to work, having been disabled in the Battle of Antietam. Tullar's mother died when he was just two years old, so Grant had no settled home life until he became an adult. Yet from a life of sorrow and hardship, he went on to bring joy to millions of Americans with his songs and poetry.

As a child, he received virtually no education or religious training. He worked in a Bolton woolen mill and later as a shoe clerk. The last Methodist camp meeting in Bolton was in 1847, and Tullar became a Methodist at age nineteen at a camp meeting near Waterbury in 1888. He then attended the

Unlucky Civil War disabled patriotic veteran Austin Tullar named his son after General Grant. His son, Grant Colfax Tullar, became a well-known music publisher and poet.

Hackettstown Academy in New Jersey. He became an ordained Methodist minister and pastored for a short time in Dover, Delaware. For ten years, he was the song leader for evangelist Major George A. Hilton. In 1893, he helped found the well-known Tullar-Meredith Publishing Company in New York. Tullar composed many popular hymns and hymnals. One of Grant Tullar's most quoted poems is "The Weaver":

My life is but a weaving
Between my Lord and me;
I cannot choose the colors
He worketh steadily.

Oft times He weaveth sorrow
And I, in foolish pride,
Forget He sees the upper,
And I the under side.
Not til the loom is silent
And the shuttles cease to fly,
Shall God unroll the canvas
And explain the reason why.

The dark threads are as needful
In the Weaver's skillful hand,
As the threads of gold and silver
In the pattern He has planned.

He knows, He loves, He cares,
Nothing this truth can dim.
He gives His very best to those
Who chose to walk with Him.

BOLTON'S INSTRUMENTS OF WAR

The drum is not a pretty instrument; it is an instrument of war. The drum is simple, prehistoric and used in various forms and combinations in nearly every culture. The needs of extended military marches, encampment discipline and warfare encouraged the development of fife and drum music in Europe in the 1400s. The American Patriots and the British army faced off against each other while directing their military maneuvers with this music. Today, fife and drum music is closely associated with the birth of America.

The heaviest concentration of fife and drum corps happens to be in Connecticut. There are only four fife and drum corps in the United States that continue as part of actual military organizations—one is the Second Company Governor's Footguard in Connecticut. The oldest actual continuing military cavalry in America is Sheldon's Light Horse (Dragoons), which was formed in Connecticut during the Revolution. Bolton's David Loda and Jamie Klim are dragoons.

A regiment of eight hundred to one thousand men was just about the largest military unit that could be commanded by a single voice. It would typically have sixteen to twenty fifers and drummers, who sometimes banded together to form a regimental band. The musicians provided music for the army on the march and to broadcast when to get up, breakfast, assemble, lunch, sup and lights-out. The tattoo (the last music of the day) was a signal for the taverns to turn off the beer spigots so the soldiers would retire for the night. It consisted of the fifes and drums parading up and down the streets. They would conclude the tattoo with a beautiful hymn.

Fife and drum signals were used to position the troops on and off the battlefield. Musical signals were given to make troop formations turn in various ways, halt, march, extend and retract lines. An important daily duty was the parade, where troop strength and equipment could be inspected, awards and punishments conferred, orders given and formal announcements issued. Fife and drum music continued to be used by the American military into the American Civil War. But the increased scale of battles required a louder instrument, so the bugle replaced the fife.

Drum competitions were held after the Civil War. Sidney Basney, the lead drummer for the Bolton Drum Corps in the late 1890s, was a black man who could play more beautifully than anyone of his time. Curiously, however, he received seven second-place awards and never won a first prize. In 1895, the economy was beginning to pull out of a depression when, on August 28, the tenth annual convention of the Connecticut Fifers and Drummers Association was held in Meriden. Fourteen corps participated. Once again, Basney, now sixty-one years old, painted the afternoon breezes with his drum cadences. Hardened Civil War veterans were entranced by his drumming skills and brushed aside a tear or two. Again, people agreed he was probably the best in America, but the judges gave him the second place. How could that be? The judges sat behind a solid wall to be certain they could not see who was playing. The names of the contestants were not told to the judges, they were just rated by the order in which they played. Use of rudiments (prescribed exercises) allowed for the objective comparisons of skill. Yet Bolton's Sidney Basney still got second place!

Battlefield commanders wanted short, simple drum codes that were easily understood and to the point. Basney created music with grace notes, flams and taps; he held back, sweetening the attacks of the prominent, left-hand lead and seven-stroke roll. But such phrasing was not militarily useful because openly spaced notes were best understood in battle. No, the judges did not discriminate against Sidney Basney. First place went to the most militarily useful presentation. Second place went to the most skilled and beautiful presentation, because the drum is not a pretty instrument; it is an instrument of war.

THE RAILROAD ERA

The railroad was the first private, limited-access mass transportation system. By 1833, plans for a rail line from Hartford to Providence were beginning to emerge. Businessmen dreamed of a New England railroad to follow the prosperous alignment of towns along the Revolutionary Road that went through Bolton. In 1847, the Hartford & Providence Railroad was chartered and quickly consolidated into the Hartford, Providence & Fishkill Railroad (HP&F).

The HP&F began operating between Hartford and Willimantic in 1849. The Norwich Turnpike railroad crossing grade of Watrous Road was dangerously steep, making it difficult for carriages to accelerate and clear the tracks. Watrous Road was therefore closed and the Norwich Turnpike railroad crossing was moved to Steeles Crossing Road. There was a telegraph office located there and school children could catch a free ride to class. By 1855, the HP&F had expanded quickly to Waterbury. The deep whooshing sound of the whistle filled the valleys, giving everyone a chance to snap the reins of their horses if they were running late. Neighing horses increased their gait in excitement. A cloud of smoke bellowed from the steam engine as the train hissed into the Bolton depot in the notch. Young horses bolted and reared up at the sights, sounds and smells. Tromping oxen with thundering wagons full of supplies plodded up to the loading dock as working men clamored endlessly in the background.

But the HP&F was running on borrowed money and borrowed time; it went into receivership in 1857. After a series of bankruptcies and mergers, the

Marvin Howard would transport goods between the railroad station, local stores and factories. Here he is delivering lye and other goods to the Soap Works, a small factory at Bolton Notch.

NYNH&H train crew poses on the new line that ran through Bolton.

This was a tough bunch of big-handed, iron-hammering rail men who maintained the rail track through Bolton and other towns.

The railroad executives found Bolton Notch and the pond so attractive that they built a place they could go to for retreats. Today the Bolton Conservation Commission organizes hikes into this once privately owned region of Freja Park and Bolton Notch State Park.

powerful New York, New Haven & Hartford Railroad emerged, foundered in 1900 and then reemerged.

The railroad executives noted the beautiful features of Bolton Notch and built a clubhouse accessible only by rail to enjoy the fish and wildlife. The site was also used by prominent guests and was a place to discuss business in a relaxed atmosphere. It was a short walk from the notch itself.

However, competition began to grow for the railroads as a national highway system of good roads was adopted. After World War II, larger trucks on the limited-access highways began to win the competition. The final blow to Bolton's railroad dream came with a hurricane in 1956 that created a record flood that took out a critical railroad bridge in Putnam, Connecticut. That closed the chapter on the New England railroad through Bolton. The railroad property is now a Connecticut greenway approximately one hundred feet wide, connecting several Bolton hiking trails, wetlands and wildlife habitats.

THE LESS DELICATE ARTS OF RURAL BOLTON LIFE

Their whips were impressive instruments of encouragement, guidance and motivation. Bullpunchers, with little more than sheer muscle and sinew, were the tough, rock-hard men who helped wrestle logs out of the Bolton woods and stones from the Bolton Quarry and then hauled them to build and heat the city of Hartford.

The French army brought approximately 1,600 oxen pulling four hundred wagons through Bolton in 1781 and on their return trip in 1782. They also had several hundred horses, primarily for riding and pulling carriages. The animals were put to maximum use. When an ox or horse died, it usually was from old age and exhaustion, so they naturally had rather tough meat. The day they died, the army and families on the trail had beefsteak served after the dead ox or horse was tenderized. That is where the expression "to beat a dead horse" comes from. They beat the dead horses and dead oxen to tenderize them before preparing them for dinner.

By 1850, New England was in the midst of the Industrial Revolution. The highlands of Bolton were the watersheds that supplied power to run mills in Tolland and Windham. As a result, Bolton was without Hop River daylight water power to do much more than run a few mills. Shoddy Mill was a factory for recycling old woolen clothing that rag pickers brought in by the wagonload. Stony Road had a small sawmill site, along with Camp Johnson.

Top: George Stanley with his oxen on Hop River Road in the early 1900s, hauling logs through Bolton to Hartford.

Bottom: Marvin Howard and his team of oxen in a 1920 photo at Notch Road, carting goods across the Notch Road wooden bridge to the railroad depot.

The primary power and moving force in Bolton in those days was the ox. Oxen were gelded bulls, not known for their speed. It was the bullpuncher who persuaded the oxen to move, and he was not delicate about it. After the train whistle, the loudest sound in Bolton, in those days, was the bellowing of the bullpuncher as he goaded and prodded the phlegmatic former bulls. The bullpuncher had his plugs of chewing tobacco, his whiskey and his own type of profanity. They were a colorful, roaring breed who could spit brown sticky tobacco juice with what local children considered enviable accuracy. Curious children usually kept their distance and learned not to taunt the bullpunchers.

A road grader in those days consisted of at least four oxen pulling a large quarry stone that leveled the road. The grader gradually lowered the road level, so that over time dirt roads would move up to four hundred feet sideways as the bullpuncher sought better road drainage.

The bullpuncher was often tempestuous and impatient, and if the load was great he might run up and down the long line of oxen, jabbing them

Kneeland Jones, who farmed at Bolton Center, was the last Bolton ox driver to enter ox-draw fair competitions. Here he farms the old way in the 1930s, before there were hay bailers. He skillfully stacks the hay that his helpers throw to him as the oxen move slowly on autothrottle.

with his goad stick while furiously roaring insults at them. He always kept an eye on the restless brutes, because with a swing of the ox's head or the lashing out with its hind leg, a man could be crippled or killed. The bullpuncher knew that when an ox's eyes rolled back, he had to jump back since the beast would then kick out. The oxen had to be tough to survive, but the men had to be even tougher.

Lumber dealer George Stanley and ox driver Marvin Howard had to be tougher than their oxen, too. Children showed great respect for their special communication and motivational skills. Oxen, more than horses, were used to pull plows and wagons because they were steady and moved at the right speed for our rough roads and fields. Horses were primarily for riding on wider, smoother roads, where speed was an option. With the invention of the internal combustion engine, the days of oxen were numbered.

Richard Rose likes to tell a story about farmer Kneeland Jones, the last ox-pull county fair champion from Bolton to enter his oxen in the sled-pulling contests. It is the story about when Richard learned to keep his distance. Richard had a small bicycle as a young teenager and one day he saw Kneeland driving his team down Bolton Center Road. Pedaling feverishly, he almost made one pass around Kneeland and his team when Kneeland began bellowing at him. That only tempted Richard to try a second pass. As soon as he started the second pass, Richard felt the whip snap much, much too close for comfort, and was off like a bolt. Yes the whip was indeed an impressive instrument of guidance and motivation.

Part VI

The Belles of Bolton

U ncas, well before Lincoln, knew that a culture doesn't grow old and decay because it has existed a certain number of years; it grows old and dies from the inside when it deserts its ideals. The years may add patina, but deserting one's ideals impoverishes the soul of a people, tribe, community or nation.

Today we try to live our promised future in the present. As long as we breathe, Bolton will fight for the future, that radiant future in which people, strong and beautiful, remain stewards of the land and of their heritage. Bolton will remain young and innocent as long as it remains open to what is beautiful and good, and receptive to the messages of nature, history and God.

THE SUMNERS OF BOLTON

The name Sumner is well known not only in Bolton, but also in the history of Connecticut and the United States. The Sumner family includes a long lineage of patriots, diplomats and statesmen. Members of the family have been prominent in all the professions, especially in business and in finance. On December 25, 1977, the *Hartford Courant* magazine featured a story about the fiftieth anniversary of the largest bequest for paintings ever made to the Wadsworth Athenaeum. The 1927 donation of nearly $2 million was given in the names of the wives of the two Bolton brothers, Francis and George Sumner. The Ella Gallup Sumner and Mary Catlin Sumner Collection remains the most extensive collection of paintings at the Wadsworth Athenaeum today.

The Connecticut Sumner family traces back to William Sumner, born at Bicester in Oxfordshire, England, in 1605. Reverend Henry Peterson Sumner was born June 10, 1773, the ninth child in a family of eleven children. On September 11, 1798, Mr. Sumner married Mary Goslee, daughter of Timothy Goslee, of Glastonbury. Reverend Sumner was a clergyman of the Methodist church, and he initially traveled his circuit on horseback. He was a prominent member of the church conference. He became the minister and a key manager of the Gay City community on the border of Hebron and Bolton. Reverend Sumner died January 18, 1838, and his widow passed away at the homestead (Bolton Heritage Farm) on August 9, 1875.

Their son, John Wesley Sumner, was the eighth of eleven children. He was born September 16, 1812. He was the first Sumner to reside at what is now Bolton Heritage Farm. He was a prominent Democrat and represented Bolton in the General Assembly in 1877 and 1878.

On November 23, 1836, John Wesley Sumner married Mary, daughter of George Gleason of Glastonbury. Their son, George Gleason Sumner, was born January 14, 1842. Mary Ella was born April 24, 1848. Their son, Francis Chester Sumner, was born June 8, 1850. George, Ella and Frank received their early education in the public schools of Bolton. Mary died at age twenty-eight on October 6, 1876. George Gleason Sumner married Ella Gallup and became a well-known lawyer and orator. He was a recognized leader in the Connecticut State Democratic Party and held various local offices in Hartford where he became mayor, and where he served in the positions of state representative and state senator. In 1883, he was elected the lieutenant governor of Connecticut. He outlived his wife and two children, and when he died on September 8, 1906, his fortune went to his dear brother Frank.

Francis (Frank) Chester Sumner began his business career as messenger for the Hartford Trust Company on February 1, 1871. Frank had a natural talent for banking and finance, and he made every effort to master its intricacies with intelligence and care. He advanced rapidly, and in 1886, he was made treasurer of the company and a member of the board. Frank Sumner was also a trustee of the Mechanics Savings Bank.

On June 17, 1896, Frank Chester Sumner married Mary L. Catlin, daughter of George S. Catlin of Hartford. Like his father and brother, Frank Sumner always took an active interest in public affairs, and was a prominent member of the Democratic Party. In the spring of 1905, he became a member of the Hartford City Water Board. He also served on the common council.

ELLA GALLUP SUMNER

MARY CATLIN SUMNER

1878 - GEORGE G. SUMNER - 1880

FRANK C. SUMNER
Sec'y-Treas, Hartford Trust Company

The names Ella Gallup Sumner and Mary Catlin Sumner are well known at the Wadsworth Atheneum. Their husbands, George G. and Frank C. Sumner, received their educations in one-room schoolhouses in Bolton and made fortunes that later went to an endowment that is still purchasing oil paintings.

Top: Charles F. Sumner's house, shown in winter.

Bottom: A picture of Ella and Jeanette Sumner leaving the house in 1919, after a heavy snowstorm of the kind that comes about every one hundred years.

Edna Sumner in her one-horse shay in front of her house on Bolton Center Road, circa 1938.

It was the fashion in the late 1800s to dress little boys and girls in the same clothes. Charles F. Sumner became deputy treasurer of the State of Connecticut. Keeney Hutchinson was the Bolton town treasurer in the 1940s.

For many years, Frank Sumner devoted much time to educational matters. He was a member of the jury commission in Hartford from its conception. From June 1899 until his death, he was a commissioner of the Connecticut River, Bridge and Highway Commission, under whose direction the first concrete bridge was built across the Connecticut River. The bridge bore his name. He was active in prison reform and was a director of the state prison from 1893 until his death. He was a director of the Connecticut Humane Society, the Hartford Free Dispensary, the Hartford Chamber of Commerce and the Hartford Hospital.

George Sumner spent most of his time at the homestead in Bolton, the Minister's Farm. The farm was kept in his mother's name, Mary Gleason Sumner, the entire time. His brother Frank often stayed there as well with his wife Mary. Before they modernized the colonial exterior, two small barns set behind the house with the farm's stone-lined country lane turning where the current barn is and exiting on the current driveway. That country lane is probably the original colonial road that took a gentle path up the hillside. They then constructed a large barn and a house addition that both extended over the current driveway, blocking the country lane. George was very active in Bolton. Frank Sumner owned and took care of the farm and then it went to his cousin Charles Fletcher Sumner Jr., who then sold it to George O. Rose in 1922. George Rose built the milking parlor and silo. The Town of Bolton bought the farm in 2000, after archaeological digs in 1998 established it as Bolton's Revolutionary War campsite. It is now called Bolton Heritage Farm.

Another son of Reverend Henry Sumner, Dr. Charles Fletcher Sumner, born in 1817, married Josephine White and moved in 1834 to the Jabez White house in Bolton (currently the Jonathan Treat house). He served twenty years on the school board, and saved and wrote about much of Bolton's history. Their children were Charles Fletcher Jr. and Elizabeth. Their son, Charles Fletcher Sumner Jr., was born in 1864, and was at one time the deputy treasurer of the state of Connecticut.

Fletcher married Edna Conklin of Hartford in 1900. Charles and Edna had three daughters: Elizabeth, Ella and Jeanette. Their daughter Elizabeth Sumner married Charles Ubert and had two daughters, Genevieve and Cynthia. Genevieve, now Genevieve Robb, spent much of her youth in Bolton and is currently a member of the Bolton Historical Society.

The bequest of the combined fortunes of Bolton scions, George and Frank Sumner, was made in the names of their beautiful wives, the Belles of Bolton, whom they loved dearly. Both George and Frank were known for their generosity, philanthropy and deep commitment to their dual communities

The Sumner family on a winter day in the 1930s. The children are Cynthia Ubert and Genevieve Ubert. The adults from left are Charles Ubert, Edna Sumner, Elizabeth Sumner Ubert, Ella Sumner, Jeanette Sumner and Charles F Sumner. Genevieve is currently a member of the Bolton Historical Society.

of Bolton and Hartford. The next time you visit the Wadsworth Athenaeum, look for the Ella Gallup Sumner and Mary Catlin Sumner Collection and see the major contribution that Bolton's Sumner family made to one of the finest art museums in America.

RUTH'S STORY: SUMMER DAYS ON BOLTON LAKE

Here is a page in the life of Ruth Johnson Converse, who as a child spent many happy summers on Bolton Lake. Ruth, who was the grandmother of Bolton Tax Collector Lori Bushnell, left us these great memories of Bolton.

The year was around 1929 when my father hired a builder to build the cottage at Bolton Lake. The small driveway down to the cottages is now called Lakeside Lane. There were three cottages and a vacant lot next to our cottage.

My father, with my mother Lydia, and me, Ruth Johnson Converse, would drive there on what is now called Old Bolton Road, which at that time went through wetlands and marsh. At the end of the old road we came to Gowdy's gas station where my father filled his old Studebaker up with gas. Then up the hill, where we would pass a big white house on the left that was my grandparent's farm, where the veterinary hospital is today. The story goes that grandmother would not move there because Bolton had no electricity and she didn't want to go back to gas lamps. So grandfather, Mr. Brink, with the help of the Cheneys, for whom he worked, brought electric light poles from Manchester up to Bolton to the farm. This was the first electric wiring in Bolton.

We would pass the Rainbow Club, as it was called back then. It was painted in stripes of different colors to represent a rainbow. It later became Fiano's and then Georgina's Restaurant. On the left was Bolton Notch Pond with the railroad tracks running alongside of it. The train station was there and when the trains came through, their whistles could be heard echoing way up at the lake.

Mr. Haling owned the Bolton Notch quarry that built many buildings in and around Hartford. On to the left was the Bolton Notch Mountain known for Squaw Cave. The next street on the left was Vernon Street. It had quite a few cottages built on the shores of Bolton Lake.

Next on the left was a hotel owned by Mr. and Mrs. Haley. On the main floor was an ice cream and candy store that we kids enjoyed. There was a brown barn on the side of the yard. Mr. Haley cut ice from the lake in the winter and stored it in the barn with piles of sawdust to keep it from melting. My father always stopped to get a block of ice for our icebox. The lake had no electricity, so we had to keep things cold in iceboxes. Mr. Haley also rented rowboats for fishing and for pleasure.

There were about four cottages on the left on the lake before we turned into our lane. The Thompsons owned the farm and a big white house on the hill above the lane where the cottages were. Some hot weekends my folks, Phil and Lydia Johnson, and I would get everything ready in the car to drive up to the lake to go swimming to cool off. Sometimes when we got there the lake would be dry. The Willimantic Thread Mill would use lake water for their power and empty the lake. However, it was a good time for all the men to go into the dry lake and clean up all the cedar stumps. They would

Ruth Converse provided her family portrait circa 1925, taken when she was the child experiencing the trip that she described out to Bolton Lake. The entire picture frame and setting shows printed scenes typical of the memories people kept at that time.

put them in a huge pile and have a big bonfire. The lake was Cedar Swamp at one time, because it had so many cedar trees. The lake was usually full with good clean fresh water and a delight to jump in to swim. My father bought me water wings to teach me how to swim. They were made of heavy material with a wooden mouthpiece to blow them up. Families had wooden rowboats and some had small engines on the back. Men used them to troll to catch their fish.

A friend and I would walk the stone wall in front of the cottages all the way around to the dam. Near the dam the land was all wet and marshy. From the dam we saw Mr. Hull's boathouse and all his land across from the dam. In the summertime, we would walk up the highway past the old 18th century Bolton cemetery, and come to the house where the Methodist minister lived. It had an open porch at that time where he would hang a cage with his pet parrot in it. We would call to the parrot and the parrot would answer back. We would go to the Methodist Strawberry Festival. We would eat our shortcake on Mr. and Mrs. Perrett's lawn, which was on the opposite corner from the church on South Road. They had tables and chairs set up for us to use. There was also a puppet show to watch.

Fannings Place was one of the first summer homes where guests could swim, row a boat or go out on the lower Bolton Lake, circa 1905.

There was a small meat and grocery store owned by Al Skinner on the lane that is now called North Road. The land between the lake and North Road was developed in later years to what is now Keeney Drive and the state owned the boat launch.

THE BOLTON-*TITANIC* CONNECTION

Abraham Lincoln said that we cannot escape history and, indeed, sometimes we seem to be pursued by it. Mike Foley, owner of the Foley Baker organ company once located at 1212 Boston Turnpike in Bolton, bought the building from AT&T in 1979. At the time, he was told by AT&T that it had a *Titanic* connection. When the ship *Titanic* sank, word was radioed to London and then to France, where it was transmitted at the speed of light in an underwater cable to Orleans and Massachusetts (Cape Cod), then to a repeating station in the basement of his building here in Bolton and finally on to New York City. The messages were in Morse code and the signals were weak when they came into the repeating station. The weak signal drove a switch that repeated the signal, leaving the building but with a much higher voltage. High voltage and low amps traveled farther but sparks flied in the switches and it could sound like Frankenstein's lab.

In Mike Foley's voice, you could almost hear the mournful sound of the *Titanic* as its foghorn pealed out a warning in the cold fog of the North Atlantic. What strange circumstance of fate could possibly bring Bolton into this picture? So began an investigation of the Bolton-*Titanic* Connection.

Mike said that the cable conduits for the lines were now all empty. His building dated from 1939, so how could it have been involved with the *Titanic*, which sank in 1912? In 1912, the roads of Bolton were still all dirt. Mike said he had written to the French cable station that had built the line, but did not get a response. He asked me if I could find out if the connection existed in 1912.

The Internet listed the French Cable Station Museum as being located on Cape Cod in Orleans, Massachusetts. It was an amazing feat for the French to operate a transatlantic cable with the limited technology they had over a century ago. Donald Howe, the engineer who keeps the museum equipment in running order, said their station was built in 1890, and that he believed they once had an inland line but didn't know any of the details. He invited me to look through the museum files, but that meant a wait of several months. However, when he heard that the sinking of the *Titanic*, his museum and Bolton had a possible connection, his voice sparked with curiosity.

Miss Loomis is shown with her horse and buggy. She was postmaster beginning in 1918. It was a common practice for her to pick up the mail at the train station at 8:00 a.m. and then distribute it from her home, which sometimes served as a grocery store as well. Miss Loomis sold penny candy on the side. At times, there were as many as three postmasters in Bolton simultaneously.

F.J. Olds delivered choice meats to the home. Many people had no transportation, so bread, pastries and meats were often delivered. Residents who did not have cows bought milk from the other local farmers and made cream, ice cream, butter and buttermilk.

The very next day, Donald Howe went through all the museum records himself and confirmed that, beginning in 1890, the French undersea cable took an inland route through Bolton on the Boston Turnpike. The 1939 building probably had replaced an earlier building on that site. Howe confirmed that the line was in service at the time of the *Titanic* and through World War II. At some point in time, AT&T began providing a leased line. In 1979, the Orleans station was bought from the French by townspeople to preserve their heritage. That was the same year Foley Baker bought the Bolton AT&T property. Mike Foley's Bolton connection to the sinking of the *Titanic* was true. Who knows what other news sparked its way beneath the soil of Bolton Notch?

THE DEW DROP HISTORY MYSTERY

In the 1800s, Bolton was bypassed by the Industrial Revolution and gradually lost more than 50 percent of its population to the westward migration, falling to only 448 people by 1920. There was no significant development for almost a century, and poverty preserved Bolton's heritage until the 1920s, when a new wave of farmers and people arrived after fleeing war-torn Europe.

It was not until 1940 that Bolton had as many people again as it had in 1808, when Bolton split to form the town of Vernon.

Population

Year	Bolton	Vernon
1782	1,081	—
1790	1,292	—
1800	1,452	—
1810	700	827
1820	731	966
1840	739	1,430
1850	600	2,009
1900	457	8,483
1920	448	8,898
1940	728	8,978
1950	1,279	10,115
1960	2,933	16,961
1990	4,575	40,822
2000	5,017	43,026

Top: The Bolton railroad station was located at Bolton Notch, next to the pond.

Bottom: The Dew Drop Inn was located on Bolton Lake.

Early photographs from several sources and several Bolton historical postcards from about the early 1900s have three figures in them, sometimes hardly noticeable, far in the distance. These three young women must have posed for half of the known scenic postcards made in Bolton. John Knoll took many pictures like these in 1919.

In the period of the late 1800s and early 1900s, it was fashionable to have inns with names that were puns. A common humorous name for a new inn in 1900, for instance, was "Nowhere Inn Particular." Some of the pictures depicted the inn on Bolton Lake as the "Dew Drop Inn," a Victorian pun meaning, "please do drop in."

The census of 1900 reveals that about 75 percent of Bolton's population had pulled up stakes and moved west. The west was tamed and traveling circuses were popularizing cowboy and Indian shows. The staff running the inns during this period frequently called themselves "Inn-dians" or just "Inndians." Inns were for rest and relaxation. Route 44 (named in 1922) was then called the Boston Turnpike, the main road between Hartford and Boston. It was in 1913 that the Norwich and Boston Turnpikes first met in Bolton Notch and Route 6 was established as a national highway following the path of the Norwich Turnpike.

The three young ladies in the photos pose at the Bolton Notch railroad station and on the porch of the Dew Drop Inn. The girl in the center is believed to be Mildred England. The girl on the far right is believed to be Ester Sturgeon. Anna, on the left in a white jumper, later became Anna Grimason and the executive secretary to Howell Cheney of the Cheney Silk Mills. Anna was born in 1904. If you look closely at one photo, it is clear that Mildred is holding a cigar in her right hand. The other two ladies are striking a pose in their latest bobbed hairdos. Anna later claimed that Mildred got sick from smoking that cigar. They have an air of independence and liberation about them, especially considering the repressed period they had lived through. In 1872, Susan B. Anthony had been arrested and stood trial in Rochester, New York, for the illegal act of attempting to vote in the presidential election. In 1878, a women's suffrage amendment was introduced in the United States Congress. The wording was unchanged forty-one years later in 1919, when the amendment finally passed both houses. The Nineteenth Amendment was ratified by the states on August 26, 1920.

It was 1919, and America was about to give women the right to vote and then plunge into the Roaring Twenties and prohibition. During that time, these women would be considered courageous—"Thoroughly Modern Millie"—and in step with the times. It was also the moment in history

Mike Pesce operated a cider press on the corner of Hebron Road and Loomis Road.

Albert Lodi, Thelma Pesce Fracchia and Antoinette Pesce, with Thelma's pet goats. In 1938, Pesce's Cold Meats/Import Groceries and Tydol Gas Station opened. The store was expanded to include a package store in 1939. Country Liquors and A-1 Grocery Store are located there today.

Armando and Giovanni Pesce and Albino Varca grew produce in Bolton and sold it at the farmers' markets in Manchester and elsewhere.

Top: Norma Pesce milked the cows on her family farm.

Bottom: The family relaxes and someone snaps a picture, circa 1933.

when Bolton began to grow again as beautiful, hardworking people from Italy began revitalizing farming in Bolton.

Ghosts of Bolton, Past and Present

A few years ago, a local *Hartford Courant* writer asked about a Bolton Quarryville ghost story. We had at one time omitted stories about the ghosts of Bolton, for fear they could adversely affect the Bolton real estate market. The reporter explained that ghosts are no problem. Her house in Mansfield was haunted until she just told the ghost that he frightened her and that she wished he would stop appearing. He never appeared again! Ghosts are described as being in a state of denial, unable to accept the fact that they have died and should move on. You'd think they would eventually notice their clothing was very much out of fashion. But God help us if they started to dress like us. Then you would not easily know who the ghosts were. If you encounter a ghost or a ghostly phenomenon in Bolton, just keep your wits about you. But before you read further, are your doors and windows locked? Are all the lights on? Are you sitting in the middle of your bed with your feet off the floor, so that if something is below the bed, it can't pull you under?

Gay City Hollow rests in peace at the south side of Bolton. It was founded about 1796 by a religious order whose members believed in serving the male members whiskey before their two weekly services. This promoted good attendance and tended to enliven the meetings. The religious order built a channel in which water was said to have flowed uphill from a pond to a waterwheel that powered their mills. That frightened some workers away. Many strange things occurred in Gay City, causing the local Bolton folk to stay away generally. Abandoned by the religious order shortly after the War of 1812, the mills continued to be operated until fires mysteriously burned most of them to the ground.

The ghosts of Bolton Notch Hollow are said to affect the weather. Drivers have frequently reported their car windows misting over and sometimes freezing solid white as they pass over the abandoned railroad line in the deepest part of the notch. I know that to be a fact, for it has happened more than once to my family driving to church on Sunday morning.

Another question is who watches over the painted rock on the cliff of Bolton Notch? Who painted the flag there after 9/11? Who puts the Christmas tree and flag up on the rock? Why do so many electrical storms start in the notch and swoop down the Hop (Hope) River valley? Whose eerie voice is heard singing up on the rocks when the full moon crosses the notch on many lonely summer nights? There are ghostly stories of the dead quarrymen, Hagar the missing Dutchman and the wanderings of executed Narragansett Chief Miantonomo, all of whom had untimely deaths in Notch Hollow.

Of the twenty-six Notch Hollow buildings that still existed as late as 1913, only one remains today near Quarry Road. Notch Hollow is now a ghost of the past, existing in our imaginations and a few photographs. Most people now call it Bolton Notch, from the deep trench left by more than two hundred years of quarrying and the railroad. In the 1600s, the Mohegan Indians knew this sacred area to be the highest land in the region, dominated by an enormous, sacred flat rock, Wiashguagwumsuck, at the northwestern border of their territory.

The railroad executives built a clubhouse for themselves and their influential friends at the west end of Notch Hollow. The trains would stop there when signaled, as well as at the usual stop at the station in the notch. Steam from the train would condense and sometimes fog up or even frost over the station windows and nearby car windows in the winter. One story goes that four lawyers who were wheeling and dealing in the booming thread mill industry had met at the clubhouse to strategize. A big hulking man entered from the howling snowstorm and silently stood before the clubhouse fire, rubbing his enormous hands, trying to warm himself. They could not see his face but worried that the stranger may have overheard some of their schemes. Wondering if he was from Willimantic, they demanded, "Where are you from, sir?" Suddenly the room was as cold as all outdoors. The man spun around, and with eyes like burning coals he snarled, "From Hell, where you four are going." Then he threw open the door and disappeared back into the swirling snow and was never seen again.

The ghost train has been reported in many towns along both abandoned and operating rail lines. The legend says that the ghost train's steam, wheels and carriages make not a single sound as they sweep along on invisible rails. Sometimes people in Bolton have seen a steamy white mist sweep down the greenway trail as though it was from an old ghostly steam train. Could the sudden condensation on car windows in the summer, and the sudden winter frosting-over of car windows as cars cross the abandoned rail line at the notch, be caused by the steam of Bolton's passing ghost train?

Martin Luther, the Catholic priest who started the Reformation, threw an ink pot at an apparition one night in Wartburg Castle. Today you can visit his room and still see the ink splatter on the wall. But today, seeing apparitions doesn't look good on your job resume, unless perhaps your name is Ed or Lorraine Warren. This husband and wife team of ghost hunters,

Motorists entering Bolton Notch from the Hop River valley sometimes experience a fogging or icing-over of their windshields, even though no steam trains have used the rail bed for half a century. It has been referred to as the ghost train phenomenon.

primarily associated with *The Amityville Horror*, has visited Bolton and wants you to know they will come again if you need their help.

The January 2001 meeting of the Bolton Historical Society brought out spontaneous discussion of the past and present ghosts of Bolton. One house in town boasts of a ghost who is dressed as a soldier, who sometimes descends the staircase on moonlit nights. Residents of another house have seen a Civil War–era woman wearing an outfit complete with hoop skirt and bonnet. Still another house had old unexplained gravestones lying face down in the walkway around the house. But the most recent story is that of Bolton residents who purchased a historic home and decided to have it checked out by the well-known ghost hunters, Ed and Lorraine Warren. The jaw of their real estate agent dropped when she met them. The Warrens walked all around the house, and then suddenly Lorraine stopped and said she felt something strange in the sitting room. She told everyone to wait outside and she went in and closed the door behind her. The hair on the back of the home buyer's neck stood up. Lorraine then emerged from the room and said there was no ghost but a presence. The owners later learned that the previous owner, an elderly woman, spent much of her time alone in that room before she died.

Sue Gorton sent me a poem she wrote long ago that suggests that the American Indian maiden Wunnee could be the one behind many unexplained pranks and other happenings in Bolton. Wunnee could be taking revenge or looking for Peter Hagar. Sue and Bob Gorton lived on Brandy Street, and for many years Bob was the chairman of the Bolton Planning Commission. In her clever poem, she mentions some familiar names: Doc Olmsted, Kris Pelletier, Grant Davis, Tom and Marilee Manning, Ray Halsted and Phil and Pat Dooley. BOMARCO stands for Bolton Married Couples, a social club in town. Thank you, Sue, for allowing me to use your poem:

"The Ghost of Bolton Notch"
By Sue Gorton

An Indian maiden named Wunnee
Was in love with a Bolton man.
Folks cried "Miscegenation!"
And said "Your wedding is banned!"
So maid and lover ran away
Pursued by the biased lot.
They fled to the east and lived in a cave
In the hills at Bolton Notch.
The man was wounded by the crowd
(I think that he was shot.)
She nursed him with skill but still he died
In the cave at Bolton Notch.
The maiden was never seen again
Though long the crowd did watch.
They say she's still there to this day
In the cave at Bolton Notch.
She does come out from time to time
With revenge for the wedding they botched.
She isn't mean, just troublesome.
That Ghost of Bolton Notch.
The ghost is seen on Halloween
In the graveyard on the hill.
Doc Olmsted across the road just might
Draw shades and write his will.
Kris was working on a quilt

With her fabrics divided by swatch.
All her blues were turned to pinks
By the Ghost of Bolton Notch.
She took Grant's hammer up a tree
And hid it in a crotch.
This is the sort of mischief done
By the Ghost of Bolton Notch.
The Mannings we know are singers,
Both Tom and Marilee.
The Ghost has been known to hide their books.
They must sing from memory.
Ray Halsted disassembled
A precious antique watch.
One of the gears just disappeared
With the Ghost of Bolton Notch.
Sue was doing calligraphy when
The ink fell out in a blotch!
This catastrophe could only be
By the Ghost of Bolton Notch.
She went to a party at the Dooleys'.
Changed all the wine to scotch.
BOMARCO then was plastered by
The Ghost of Bolton Notch.

And so, men, if your wives keep buying you new things that you wouldn't be caught dead wearing, act a little more lively and try something new. She could be just trying to save you the embarrassment of asking to take your pulse.

Perhaps these stories have unsettled you or perhaps one of them seems too close to home and you suddenly noticed your clothing is very much out of fashion. For those Bolton ghosts reading this over your shoulder right now, I leave this Irish blessing: "May you be three days in heaven before the devil knows you're dead!"

BOLTON'S MYSTERIOUS ROVING ISLANDS

On Monday, February 28, 1955, on the fourth page of the *Bridgeport Telegram*, there appeared an article titled "Crane, Bulldozer Tear Apart Roving Island in Bolton Lakes." The action was taken under the supervision of the State Board of Fisheries and Game. The floating island measured 125 feet long,

75 feet wide and 7 feet thick. It had supported cedar trees (one eight yards tall) that served as masts and sails to drive the island around Bolton Lake. It had become a favorite private spot for young Bolton boaters, explorers and lovers.

Bolton Lake was created in the mid-1800s as part of a system to provide water power to the mills of Willimantic before electricity. As darkness descended, factories would close shop so the lake outlet in Bolton was closed earlier, raising the water level. Then, as daylight approached, the lake sluice gates would be opened, doubling the normal flow rate in the rivers powering Willimantic's Industrial Revolution. That was known as Connecticut ingenuity.

Bolton's roving islands were born when vegetation deposits created a layer of peat that had sufficient buoyancy to tear itself free from the bottom of the lake. Longtime lakeside resident Grant Davis noticed that they seemed to occur when the lake level changed. On occasion, he's witnessed the lake giving birth and has had to raise his sailboat's dagger keel in those areas where infant roving islands were not yet fully surfaced. In the last ten years, he has seen one island about seven yards across and a smaller one about a yard or more across. Native Americans called them "trembling earth," referring to the way they shook when walked upon.

Davis believes that lower lake levels decrease the overburden of the water that normally holds the peat down and compresses it. A lower lake level allows the peat to expand, increasing its buoyancy. Once part of the peat begins to tear away from the bottom, the water gets under it and there is no longer any overburden, just pure buoyancy force. Heavy soils drop away and a new roving island is born. Land plants like winterberry holly, high bush blueberry, arrowhead, fern and broad-leafed cattail then take root and hold the island together. The island moves about with roots dangling downward like the tentacles of a large lake creature feeding beneath the surface. The islands may also be blown into shallow areas and can reattach for years.

In the rising evening mist, a roving island could be a haunting sight. They were primal forces, silently creeping about the lake, obeying only natural laws of wind and water currents. As the Bolton Lake population grew, one very large roving island seemed to protest and sheared off more and more docks. Perhaps it had acquired some of the earth and spirit of the Native Americans interred beneath the lake. It would park itself wherever it pleased—it was just too bad if it chose your sandy beach as its new resting spot!

Soon this mother of all roving islands seemed to be friendless. No one had anything good to say about roving islands on February 28, 1955, when Bolton's largest recorded roving island trembled its last time and was laid to rest.

Part VII

Renaissance Bolton

Bolton needs to have different ideals from metropolitan areas. In the metropolis, before people enter their home, they scrape the city streets off their shoes. When someone moves to Bolton, they need to scrape the city off their shoes. Lighted ball fields, city sewers and city water are wonderful and there are another ten million city folk that could and would just love to move to Bolton if Bolton only had them. But that would mean Bolton would first have to give up the stars and the wild natural things. Then Bolton would give up the close sense of community, public safety and quality schools.

A town is defined not by its geography but by the character and spirit of its people. Yet in the case of Bolton, the land has dressed itself up in such attractive, light, spirited and innocent attire that we, like the French and Continental armies before us, have been seduced and behave all the more respectfully and gallantly for it. After the Revolution, time skipped by, leaving Bolton attired much like it was in its colonial youth. Perhaps the reason time has been so kind to Bolton was to save the town until its people grew to appreciate it and to value its historic and natural heritage. And so the ideals of the people of Bolton are about preserving the beauty and virtues of the land in this ancient eastern gateway to the Connecticut River valley that has become the western gateway to scenic eastern Connecticut. It is a rebirth of Bolton, the town for all seasons.

BOLTON'S WORLD WAR II VIGILANCE

On December 7, 1941, Japan attacked Pearl Harbor and 2,403 Americans lost their lives. On September 11, 2001, 2,940 citizens of several nations lost their lives when the World Trade Center towers fell. Both acts of infamy came from the air and without warning. The images were eerily similar. Ships or skyscrapers were turned into huge burning torches. They would crumble as black billowy smoke rose in great plumes through the twisted steel.

On the bridge of the USS *Arizona*, Old Glory still flew over the sunken U.S. fleet, the spirit of its seamen not defeated. And even as great plumes of acrid smoke wafted through the steel skeleton of the World Trade Center, heroic firemen raised the American flag. America's patriotic and caring spirit burned ever brighter.

The idea of flying planes into skyscrapers didn't originate with Al-Qaeda. Toward the end of World War II, an increasingly desperate Adolf Hitler ordered his engineers to develop a huge plane intended to fly missions over the Atlantic, where it would release a smaller jet bomber designed to fly near the speed of sound. Hitler referred to the plane as the "Amerikabomber." The plans for the smaller bomber it launched clearly showed that it lacked landing gear, strongly suggesting that it was a manned suicide bomb.

During World War II, Bolton citizens did not know what to expect next. A tall tower was moved from Manchester to the spot just across the green from the town hall. They built a deck around the top of it so that volunteers from Bolton and Manchester could man the tower around the clock and telephone in the position and the heading of any aircraft that were seen. Radar was only just being invented, so this was our first early warning system. The fire department had no siren alarm, so Bolton improvised. Six-feet-diameter used wheel rims from steam locomotives were hung from trees in four strategic town locations, and sledgehammers were used to beat them like gongs. One was hanging from a maple tree across from what is now the Montessori School. Automobiles had the top half of their headlights painted black so that it would be difficult for enemy planes to navigate by following illuminated roads at night. Bolton citizens practiced blackouts so that Bolton could be made invisible when the alarm was sounded.

Olive Toomey, the town clerk, was also the clerk of the rationing board. Just enough gas was allowed for people to go about their business. Scrap was collected and children saved their pennies to buy war bonds. So many people had enlisted that everyone personally knew someone who was serving. There were stories of German submarines off Connecticut's shore,

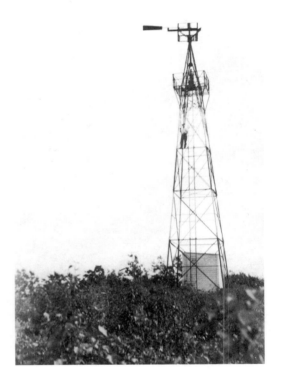

Right: This watchtower was located at Bolton Center. The town had a crew of volunteers who manned the tower and reported all aircraft that were sighted. All homes were prepared for blackouts.

Below: Bolton Center was still unspoiled after World War II.

From the top to the bottom are the Tedford, Sumner and Pesce Barns in the 1930s and 1940s.

of enemy rockets dropping on cities and of strange enemy jets and rocket planes. Anything seemed possible and the threat seemed close to home.

After the war, Albert Speer, Hitler's minister responsible for arms production, recalled in his diary Hitler's desire to attack the United States:

> *It was almost as if he was in a delirium when he described to us how New York would go up in flames. He imagined how the skyscrapers would turn into huge burning torches. How they would crumble while the reflection of the flames would light the skyline against the dark sky.*

Eternal vigilance of citizens and soldiers alike remains part of the cost of our liberty.

THE HANS CHRISTIAN ANDERSEN MONTESSORI SCHOOL

When asked why they moved to Bolton, more often than not residents report that it was for the education that their children receive. Bolton usually ranks in the top ten state school systems in achievement test scores. Bolton also has a Montessori preschool.

Maria Montessori, born in 1870 in Chiaravalle, Italy, became Italy's first female doctor in 1896. She believed that one does not teach children, but rather creates a nurturing climate in which children can teach themselves through creative activity and exploration. She visited the United States in 1913 and impressed Alexander Graham Bell, who founded the Montessori Education Association in his home in Washington, D.C.

In 1898, Reverend William McGurk bought property at Bolton Center on which his mother could run a summer home for girls with respiratory problems. During the warm months, Catholic Mass was held there every Sunday. By 1938, a larger chapel was needed because many townsfolk were attending as well. The chapel was elevated to the status of a station, and named St. Maurice. In 1950, the chapel was winterized and a permanent Catholic congregation began to grow in Bolton. By 1954, the Most Reverend Bernard Flanagan, first bishop of Norwich, raised St. Maurice to the status of parish and the Reverend J. Ralph Kelly became its first pastor. Due to its rapid growth, ground was broken for a new church in 1956.

Bolton then purchased the original chapel property, and in 1957 overwhelmingly voted to let it be used as the First Bolton Public Library. Prior to that, only a mobile library served Bolton. The American Montessori

Top: Miss Mary Clemens augmented the library with a book wagon, shown in 1938 at the home of Frank Strong.

Bottom: The Montessori School refurbished the former library building when the new Bentley Memorial Library opened next door.

Top: In the one-room schoolhouses, grades one through eight were taught. Tuition was offered for children to attend high school in other towns.

Bottom: South School in 1914.

Society was founded in 1960 as a nonprofit education society. The Hans Christian Andersen Montessori School opened in Tolland in 1964, and later moved to Bolton, renting space at St. George's Episcopal Church before finally settling at 212 Bolton Center Road, the site of Bolton's first library.

Not only do Bolton public schools rate with the best of the Connecticut private schools, but Bolton also has this private Montessori School for pre-K and kindergarten. Part of what is special about Bolton's Hans Christian Andersen Montessori School is its philosophy of learning, which has proven timeless and has spread throughout the world like a steady and shining beacon of light in education. The best schools don't teach so much as

Shown here are the first and second grade classes of 1947–48, from the one-room South School on School Road. This is the last class in Bolton to use a one-room school. The students in the front row, from left, are Bill Sauer, Richard Avery, Duncan McDonough, John Jensen, Bill Jewell and Jim Twibble. In the second row are Caroline Glenney, Ronald Carr, Bob Kuisnel, Albert Senkbeil, Kathleen McDonald, Linda Fracchetti and Doreen and Doris Sauer. In the third row are Virginia Maneggia, Joan Hathaway, Marcia Glenney, Eddie Pouech, Joan Molain, Linda Paggioli and Carl Lorentzen. In the last row are Roberta Richardson, Cecile Pepin, an unknown child, Jeanie Pouch, Lynn Broll, Nancy Maneggia, Lollie Shankin, Betty Williams, Barbara Holland, Beverly Gage and Patty Hassett. Bill Jewell's dog, Boy, is also in the front. The one-room schools were consolidated into one school in 1949, and construction began on the first brick school building, Bolton Center School.

they show their students how to learn for themselves. It isn't just the low student-teacher ratio, but rather the learning that occurs in an inquiring, cooperative and nurturing atmosphere that makes the Montessori School special. Montessori students increase their own knowledge through self- and teacher-initiated experiences. Maria Montessori recognized that students learn through the senses by manipulating materials and interacting with others. These meaningful experiences were recognized as precursors to the abstract understanding of ideas.

At the Hans Christian Andersen Montessori School, the physical, emotional, social, aesthetic, spiritual and cognitive needs and interests of the children are considered inseparable and equally important. They reinforce respect and caring attitudes for oneself, others, the environment and all life.

The family is considered an integral part of the child's total development. Taken together, this Bolton preschool education provides a diverse set of experiences which foster physical, intellectual, creative and social independence. The children leave with increased skills in social interaction, cooperative learning and emotional development.

Reverend William McGurk first bought that property at Bolton Center to help children. From that start, St. Maurice blossomed and grew. Later, on that same ground, the seeds of today's Bentley Memorial Library were sown. Today, Bolton's Hans Christian Andersen Montessori School stands there as a reminder to us that children are unique and our most precious resource.

CAMP JOHNSON

It seemed for a while that time forgot Bolton when darkness descended on Bolton's economy after the Revolution. As people began to move to Ohio and bridges were built across the rivers in southern Connecticut, the routes through the Bolton gateway from Boston and Providence became less traveled.

The Avery family bought land in 1833 on what is now Johnson Road. The Josiah B. Avery furniture shop had a turning lathe powered by a water wheel with a water drop of about ten feet. The Averys produced a wide variety of Hitchcock-type spindle back chairs, bedsteads, tables and cabinets in mahogany, oak, cherry and walnut. The U.S. census of 1850 indicated that Avery was the largest employer in Bolton (fourteen workers) and housed eight of them in his own home. The railroad of 1851 provided a convenient way for some to go to school, but it further isolated Bolton by moving commerce through without having to stop in the town. The Avery shop failed that year. The ruins of parts of the foundations, dams and mill race still remain. Unfortunately, most of the material of the ruins found their way into the house foundations, chimneys and beautiful stone walls of Bolton. The Johnson family purchased the land.

On May 10, 1948, Mr. and Mrs. Edward A. Johnson donated the property for a Boy Scout camp. It was used for a while for the Bolton community swimming program and has been used by Girl Scouts as well. Camp Johnson became the sixty-two-acre nucleus of one of Bolton's largest state-designated unfragmented wildlife habitats—a block of about two hundred acres that now includes Bolton Heritage Farm. We can feel proud to know that scouts still come to Bolton to enjoy one of our wildlife habitats. The huge tract crosses the greenway and borders the one-hundred-acre Bolton Heritage Farm. A wide variety of wildlife, including wild turkeys, black bears and bobcats, has been reported to have returned to our town. They require large blocks of contiguous habitat much like that found in this area of town.

Within the last ten years, we determined that Camp Johnson is bounded by both the pre-Revolutionary road (Johnson Road) and the Revolutionary Boston Post Road (the abandoned portion of Toomey & Stony Roads). So time has not forgotten Bolton at all; time has remembered and delivered up much of our long-lost history.

THE STAMPEDE OF JULY 4, 1950

There are times when a farmer can't rightly spit, lest he set off his entire herd of cows. What spooks a herd is often a mystery. Sometimes, though, someone comes forward years later to confess to the whole matter.

In many ways, life in Bolton following World War II was similar to life in Bolton just after the Revolutionary War. A great war had just been won, the community was close-knit, and the population was almost the same size—about 1,279 people. Townspeople who lived here in the 1950s say Bolton was a beautiful example of rural America. Most homes were large and historic, surrounded by great expanses of farmland and open space.

In 1941, when Bill Roberts brought his family to their Bolton farm on the corner of Hebron Road and Shoddy Mill Road, he joined the Bolton Volunteer Fire Department. At that time, fires were fought with bucket brigades. It was not until the end of the war in 1945 that the town bought its first pump truck. It was about then that Bill bought a dog for his wife Beatrice and their young children David and Peggy.

Where Bolton Motors stands today there was a store called Gowdy's that sold just about everything, including fireworks. In 1950, Bill Roberts had done something special. He had ordered three large professional rockets. That year, Bill decided he was going to have a blast. Bolton once had a cannon on the Bolton green but in 1835, after too much hard cider, our militia loaded the cannon with gunpowder and stuffed its mouth with stones and sod. When they fired it, that was the cannon's last blast. Little did Bill Roberts know what he was getting himself into.

As darkness descended on July 4, 1950, Bill Roberts reasoned that his neighbors had gone to bed or were away in Hartford watching the fireworks, so he would not be disturbing anyone as he set up the three huge rockets in his backyard. With buckets of water ready just in case, his family and dog watched from the side of the house. With the whoosh of the first rocket, the dog ran for cover. The yard was illuminated as the rocket stopped at its peak altitude and a beautiful flower of light spread across the sky. But then it turned into ominous silver-streaking bombs that descended two hundred feet and exploded like thunder.

When the second rocket took off, so did the dog. He bolted across Hebron Road, heading for the Masseys' cow pasture. He had always seen the cows treated with dignity and respect, which was more than the Roberts family was showing him that night. The trees were illuminated and again there was a thunderous roar from over Roberts' farm. The dog was now in the Masseys' cow pasture, and the little herd was beginning to get spooked.

Something went very wrong with the last rocket. It began to fall over just as it ignited. It narrowly missed the roof and was heading directly for the Masseys' cow pasture. The Roberts family watched nervously as it burst little more than two hundred feet above the ground and entered the cow pasture at a high speed and a low angle, overtaking the dog. Distorted by the high speed, it must have looked like a giant bobcat from hell descending on them. Then the magnesium fuses ignited and silvery claws streaked to about twenty feet above the herd, followed by an earthshaking peal of explosions. Cattle were running loose everywhere and Roberts' dog disappeared into the night.

According to Dave Roberts, he and his father helped round up the Masseys' cows that night. They were all back in the barn for milking the next morning, but the dog did not return for a week.

The Roberts family's farm was sold in 1997. Dave and Peggy Roberts Hohler were educated in the Bolton school system. Dave became a doctor in Putnam and Peggy became a vice president of State Street Corporation in Boston.

THE WISDOM OF THE ROSE FARM PRESERVATION

Bolton's effort to stem the tide of urban sprawl is perhaps the result of caring more than some developers think is wise, dreaming more than some town planners think practical, and expecting more than other towns think possible. The preservation of Bolton's quality of life is being nurtured today one acquired open space property at a time. In addition, it is believed by many that our last viable barrier to urban sprawl depends on Bolton's protecting the aquifers by maintaining sufficiently large minimum lot acreage requirements to ensure permanently safe drinking water.

There are two kinds of fortune in life. There is the normal kind we stumble through and apologize for along the way. But there is also the kind that a young boy has rounding a corner in school, colliding with a pretty girl and then, after the initial sting, profusely thanking her for the experience. It is this latter kind of fortune we have had in Bolton. Bolton, alas, collided with the Rose Farm.

Many of us watched Richard Rose working in the fields of Bolton's Rose Farm. He had childhood memories of large black circles that he saw in the plowed soil that he now knows were the locations of the large French army campfire pits at which they roasted their dinners. For seventy-eight years, his family groomed the hills with plow, disk and harrow. Then they sowed the fields and clothed the center of Bolton with the silky sheen of timothy hay, where the wind played and their cows grazed. Is it any wonder that the Rose family wanted to preserve their idyllic farm?

Reverend George Colton was the Congregational Church pastor who lived there from 1764 until 1817, and who entertained Generals Washington and Rochambeau. Today it is the very same historic vista that the Patriots saw as they prepared to camp for the night, when the summer sun was reposing. The sun's long rays of crimson light embraced the Patriots, together with the hay and stone walls, then stretched broadly and yawned across the field down to the trees. There in those fields, Patriots rested their heads and dreamed of liberty.

This farm has given its best years for us. It provided food and comfort to the Mohegan Indians. It yielded its forests to build some of our finest barns and homes. Early members of our Bolton Congregational Church cleared the land and then built the massive stone walls along the country lane. A host of Connecticut, Massachusetts and Rhode Island Patriots gazed at the farm as they passed by it along the Revolutionary Road. It provided bedding to General Rochambeau and more than five thousand rough and boisterous French, Irish, Polish, German and American soldiers during the Revolutionary War. Connecticut State Archaeologist Nicholas Bellantoni stated that Bolton Heritage Farm's French Camp Five "is the best preserved Revolutionary War site on the Rochambeau route in Connecticut."

The farm then toiled in obscurity beneath sun and storms for more than two hundred years before being rediscovered. It enchanted many passing travelers and Bolton residents. It has given us some of our best sunsets and begged Bolton to keep it whole and alive, and not ripped to pieces by bulldozers. They aren't making land anymore, and there was no land in Bolton, or in all of Connecticut for that matter, that compared with the unique heritage of the Rose Farm.

Our children deserved to have the historic Rose Farm preserved. If we were going to stop the faceless expansion of urban blight, the Rose Farm was where we had to make our stand. Letting the Rose Farm become a development would have cut the very heart out of Bolton. How often would we have had to apologize to our children and grandchildren if we had not created Bolton Heritage Farm from the Rose Farm?

But like that young boy who collided with that pretty girl, we thanked the Rose family for the good fortune they bestowed on Bolton. We made no excuses, and in a stroke of newly discovered wisdom, Bolton took the opportunity

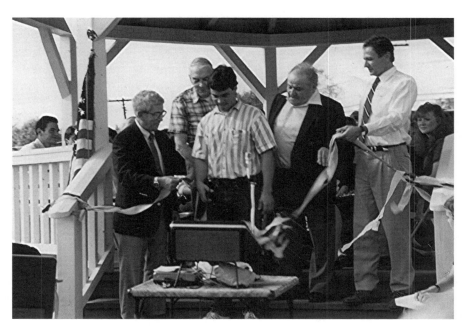

At the gazebo dedication in October 1990, Roger Barrett, whose Country Carpenters business donated the gazebo to the town, is surrounded by former first selectmen Joseph Licitra, Norman Preuss and Richard Morra. First Selectman Robert Morra is on the right.

to acquire the farm. Now we need not apologize. Instead our children and grandchildren will thank us for their opportunity to continue to enjoy Bolton Heritage Farm as perpetual fields of stones, flowers and dreams.

We were fortunate that this heritage was preserved until Bolton was wise enough and prosperous enough to protect it forever. We have the Rose Family, but especially Richard and his wife Mary Ann, to thank. It was Richard who first offered the farm through the Bolton Economic Development Commission. Richard perhaps cared a little more than some others thought practical, and risked the heat of the public spotlight perhaps more than some others considered comfortable. Thank you, Richard Rose.

Discovering the Minister's House

Just a small teaspoon of verified heritage saved Bolton Heritage Farm from development, but there are still buckets of heritage yet to be confirmed. In fact, we have just discovered another diamond in the rough.

The homes of Bolton's founders present concrete symbols of an idyllic yet very modest past. The abundance of wood and the builders' desire for sturdy construction made timber-frame houses (post-and-beam construction) most popular. In the early 1700s, Bolton's settlers were constructing what we now think of as the quintessential colonial homes. These homes were two stories high, with gables on the side and an entry door at the center. To conserve heat, a massive chimney ran through the center of the house, and the ceiling height was usually less than seven feet. Tall men had to duck their heads often in those days.

On November 11, 2005 several selectmen, historical society members and the town attorney carefully examined the Rose Farm house. That was the first time a few of us realized that the core of the Rose Farm house was probably still the original colonial structure, built around 1725. A year later, professional post-and-beam joiners and restorers inspected and agreed that the framing of the core of the house was probably the original.

In early 2008, with a grant from the Society of the Cincinnati, we were able to obtain the services of Mr. Robert P. Foley, director of preservation for the Newport Restoration Foundation, to inspect the house. He concluded that the Bolton Heritage Farm house was originally built around 1725 for the first Bolton church minister, Reverend Thomas White. Richard Rose, whose family owned the farm for seventy-eight years, confirmed that he and his father dismantled and repaired many of the rooms and found no evidence of fire anywhere in the existing house.

Standing at the W3R plaque dedication are Town Historian Hans DePold, State Commission on Culture and Tourism representative Mary Donahue, State Representative Pamela Sawyer, Second Regiment Light Dragoons First Troop Captain Sal Tarantino and Lieutenant Governor Kevin Sullivan.

Dragoon Captain Sal Tarantino talks with Rochambeau's descendant, Eric Rochambeau, and his family.

Captain Sal Tarantino, trooper Jamie Klim, trooper Dave Loda and trainer Carol Tarantino are shown in front of the Bolton Heritage Farm house, where General Rochambeau was a guest July 21, 1781, and November 4, 1782, and where General Washington dined on March 4, 1781. Dave and Jamie are from Bolton. This dragoon unit has been in service since the Revolutionary War. They often served in Bolton and accompanied General Washington.

That means we have a plurality of evidence that it is the original house where Generals Washington and Rochambeau dined on different occasions, and where Rochambeau slept and wrote to General Washington and posted one of his military reports to the French War Office. Some of the features of the rediscovered original colonial house include: very low ceilings that were in style in 1725 and very much out of style by 1830; an original attic window with some original glass, like an eight-over-twelve-paned window that dates to the early 1700s; two other windows still eighteenth century; at least one floor with wide-plank wood; many hand-hewn timbers, some panels and some early window panes in other windows; the original house stone foundation, twenty-four feet by twenty-eight feet, with the longer side facing its early driveway and down to the river; original dripstones, which were used in the 1700s to move water away from the foundation; a five sided–style ridge beam roof, which was used in the early 1700s; and evidence of the original massive colonial chimney through the original roof.

There are very few houses in America that can boast hosting nearly as many patriots and other distinguished guests during the American Revolution.

HISTORIC LEGISLATION TODAY

There is nothing that makes history come alive more vividly in our minds than the realization that we have some of the greatest examples of it right here in our community. During the American Revolution, Connecticut was the pantry and the armory for the Continental army. The threat of coastal attack by the British made the inland route, our main road through Bolton, the most heavily traveled route for deploying American troops. It linked Boston to Providence, Hartford and New York. More than five American campaigns were launched along this Revolutionary Route. The largest campaign was when General Rochambeau marched approximately five thousand French troops through our town to join General Washington and defeat the British at Yorktown, Virginia, finally ending the Revolutionary War. Twenty-three encampments were made within Connecticut towns, the best preserved one of them is here at Bolton Heritage Farm.

General Washington was a new type of warrior—a guerrilla warrior who fought with stealth, and knew that to win, the Republic only had to survive and outlast the British occupation. Washington was a general whose artillery was illusion, whose army was paid with dreams spun with hope and embroidered with daring ideas like liberty, equality and individual rights.

We must recognize that if we forget our heritage, our patriots and our allies, then we will soon forget the ideals and the principles for which they stood. If we remember them, they will continue to enrich our culture and will help us preserve our heritage. The National Park Service (NPS) has validated our heritage with a six-year study and has recommended to Congress that they create the Washington-Rochambeau Revolutionary Route National Historic Trail (W3R NHT) that includes Bolton Center Road on the route and Bolton Heritage Farm as a major Revolutionary War site.

General Washington and General Rochambeau, along with the Liberty Bell, were cast in the same fires of freedom. Their relationship was molded in Hartford and Newport, their strategy welded at Wethersfield. Their swords were wielded at Yorktown. But before they were monuments, they were men. They led their soldiers with a delight in liberty, while their voices always remained the measured voices of civilization. The Washington-Rochambeau Revolutionary Route National Historic Trail does not commemorate a battle; it commemorates the extraordinary journey that France and the United States took together as social freedom and national democracy first emerged.

The Washington-Rochambeau Revolutionary Route National Historic Trail proposal that the National Park Service has recommended to the nation will be voted on soon. The route created will be six hundred miles of history, winding from Newport, Rhode Island, through Bolton Center and on to Williamsburg and Yorktown, Virginia. Let us celebrate the unprecedented Franco-American alliance and the extraordinary efforts of Generals George Washington and Jean-Baptiste de Rochambeau to preserve that alliance in the face of seemingly insurmountable odds. Let us create a National Historic Trail along whose course we can pause and remember these heroes and their journey through colonial America to the culmination of the American Revolution at Yorktown.

Conclusion

This book is really about the ideals of a tribe, a community or a nation that make it stand for something of value, something worth keeping. And when this happens, it blossoms into cohesive cultures, civilizations, sovereign nations and lasting identities. Uncas, the American Founding Fathers and Abraham Lincoln knew what it was all about and how to make it last. They knew that a culture is destroyed from the inside when its ideals are forgotten or profaned. A culture has a history and the results are its heritage. A good culture has a heritage that its people are proud of. The American ideal of God-given rights and freedoms is so broad that almost any nontyrannical culture can thrive within it.

Bolton has awoken to its heritage, and has recognized and accepted the ideals implicit in it. That is beginning to have a profound effect. Bolton is now developing a unique and very creative culture centered on that natural and historic heritage. Once the eastern gateway of the Connecticut valley, Bolton is now becoming the western gateway of the scenic "Quiet Corner of Connecticut." Bolton is easy to find. Just drive away from the lands of lost souls and past the land of McDonald's. And there, just beyond the land of malls, you find Bolton, Conneticut.

About the Author

The author of many historical essays about Bolton, Connecticut, and the Revolutionary Road that passes through Bolton, Hans DePold has crafted a collection of true stories about ordinary people who accomplished extraordinary feats in the history of Bolton. Drawing from diaries, letters, books, newspaper articles and biographies, he paints portraits of the lives of the Native Americans, colonists, patriots, theologians, heroes and philanthropists who took the time to contribute to the greater good of those around them. Hans DePold is the Bolton town historian; Washington-Rochambeau Revolutionary Route writer for the Connecticut Society of the Sons of the American Revolution website; a *Bolton Community News* and website history writer; and founder of the Bolton Historical Society. Professionally, he is an aeronautical enginer and a computer scientist at United Technologies.

Please visit us at
www.historypress.net